Travel to Worlds Beyond

神行記

by Sheng-yen Lu

Translated by Shaun Ho and Cheng Yew Chung
Foreword by Associate Professor David B. Gray

A US Daden Culture Publication

US Daden Culture LLC
3440 Foothill Blvd.
Oakland, CA 94601
U.S.A.
Website: www.usdaden.com
Email: us.daden.culture@gmail.com

© 2010 by Sheng-yen Lu

The right of Living Buddha Lian-sheng, Sheng-yen Lu to be identified as author of this work including all translations based on his original writings, has been asserted by him in accordance with the Copyright, Designs, and Patents Act 1988.

All rights reserved. No part of this book may be reproduced in any form or by any means, electronic or mechanical, including photography, recording, or by any information storage or retrieval system or technologies now known or later developed, without permission in writing from the publisher.

Lu, Sheng-yen, 1945-
Travel to Worlds Beyond/by Sheng-yen Lu;
translated by Shaun Ho and Cheng Yew Chung;
edited by Cheng Yew Chung;
proofread by Jackie Ho.

Library of Congress Control Number(PCN): 2010929500
ISBN-13: 978-0-9841561-2-2
ISBN-10: 0-9841561-2-7
1. True Buddha School. 2. Chinese-Tibetan Buddhism.
Cover design and layout by US Daden Culture Design Team
Photograph by US Daden Culture
Set in Minion Pro 12
US Daden books are printed on acid-free paper and meet the guidelines for the permanence and durability set by the Council of Library Resources.

Printed in U.S.A.

Special Acknowledgements

The True Buddha Translation Teams (TBTTs) would like to express the highest honor and deepest gratitude to Living Buddha Lian-sheng, Sheng-yen Lu, and Master Lianxiang for their continuing support and guidance on the translation effort. Without their compassion, wisdom, blessings, and encouragement, this project would not have reached fruition.

In addition, we would like to acknowledge the diligent work put forth by the following volunteers on this project: Shaun Ho and Cheng Yew Chung (translators), Cheng Yew Chung (editor), and Jackie Ho (proofreader). We would like to thank these dedicated and selfless volunteers who have contributed their time and effort to promote the works of Living Buddha Lian-sheng, and to support the publications of the US Daden Culture.

We would also like to extend our sincere appreciation to all of the other volunteers who work behind the scenes, facilitating the translation process, and handling administrative responsibilities.

May all volunteers be blessed for their immeasurable merits; may all sentient beings benefit from the ocean of wisdom.

Table of Contents

Foreword	xi
1 Travel to Worlds Beyond - Preface	1
2 The Grand Opening Ceremony	3
3 Infinite Transformations	9
4 Rescuing a Person Committing Suicide	15
5 A Sad Love Song	19
6 Ghost Feasts	25
7 Don't Forget Your Vows	31
8 My Impression on the Welcoming of the Buddha's Finger Relic	37
9 Half-Dead Samadhi	47
10 The Five Deteriorating Signs of Heavenly Beings	53
11 Traveling over the Mountains and Rivers	59
12 The Merit of Spiritual Traveling	65
13 Grief	73
14 Spiritual Travels as Influenced by Possession	79
15 Devil Realm	85
16 The Crowd Who Prayed for Nectar	95
17 The Languages of the Heavens	103
18 Traveling in the Blood Spilled Kingdom	109

19 Protectors inside the Pores	115
20 Lingering around a Fetus	123
21 The Ecstasy Addicts in Space	133
22 Journey into the Home of a Disciple	139
23 Feast with the Mountain King	145
24 This is also Spiritual Travel	153
25 Sending a Relative to the Western Pure Land	159
26 The Writing of Listening to the Inner Voice	165
Significance of Taking Refuge	169
Glossary	173

Foreword

The True Buddha School is a new school of Buddhism that was founded by the author of this work, Grand Master Sheng-yen Lu. This tradition is "new" in the sense that it was established as a distinct buddhist tradition; Grand Master Lu and his followers have, in fact, developed an institutional basis for the tradition with remarkable speed over the past few decades. It is now a vibrant tradition with centers all over the world. However, the True Buddha School is rooted in pre-existing buddhist and Daoist traditions, and thus perpetuates venerable patterns of text and practice found throughout Indian, Tibetan, and Chinese religious tradition.

Grand Master Lu, like the founders of many other religious traditions, has had a rich spiritual life, and has cultivated many profound mystical experiences. This volume is the record of some of these experiences. As the title *Travel to Worlds Beyond* suggests, this work is an account of Grand Master Lu's personal experiences of spiritual travel, or what is often termed in the West an "out of body" experience. Grand Master Lu discusses this sort of spiritual experience at great length in this work. Not only does he relate his own spiritual journeys, but he also discusses the experience itself at length. He refers to it as a "semi-death," an intermediate state between sleeping and dying. Drawing on the Indian and Tibetan traditions, he also refers to this state as a "bardo body," the purely spiritual "mind-made body" (manomayakāya) which is the form in one exists in the dream and post-mortem intermediate state, according to those traditions.

While it is in and of itself a unique work of spiritual autobiography, it follows venerable patterns in Asian mystical literature. Grand Master Lu's account brings to mind ancient and classical Chinese accounts of celestial journeys. Descriptions of such journeys are found at the very foundation of Chinese literature, in the ancient *Chu-ci* (楚辭) poetry collection, for example. Spiritual journeys are alluded to in the classical *Zhuang-zi* (莊子), and described in much more detail in later Daoist works, such as the fourth century work *Biographies of Spirit Immortals* (神仙傳) by Ge Hong (葛洪). Similar accounts are found in the "transformation tales" (變文) of the Tang dynasty, which in turn influenced the later famous account of the celestial journey of the "Monkey King" (孫悟空) in the Ming dynasty novel *Journey to the West* (西游記). The latter, of course, maintains but a faint echo of the celestial journey genre, with most of the spiritual content replaced by martial arts fantasy, which undoubtedly contributed to the tremendous and continuing popularity of that work.

Accounts of spiritual journeys are not, of course, limited to Chinese culture. They are also found in buddhist literature. The early buddhist literature describes, for example, the Buddha's journey the the Trayastriṃśa Heaven to visit his mother. Not only the Buddha, but anyone with the requisite spiritual power can make such journeys, as we learn in *The Sāmaññaphala Sutta* and *The Kevaddha Sutta*. The stories of Mahāmoggallāna (Skt. Mahāmaudgalyāyana, Ch. 目蓮), who likewise possessed the ability to travel to different cosmic realms, were also extremely well known throughout the buddhist world.

The esoteric buddhist traditions continue this trend. The literature about the Mahāsiddhas is replete with accounts of their spiritual journeys, such as Dārika's ascent to the realm of the Ḍākas. Tibetan hagiographical literature follows this pattern; Milarepa's visionary journeys are perhaps one of the best known examples. Grand Master Lu's work, then, is a contemporary example of mystical literature in the spiritual journey genre that follows a venerable lineage of masters to whom are attributed similar mystical experiences. And one might add as well that there are also numerous examples of comparable journeys in the mystical literature of many other of the world's great religions.

This book has undoubtedly already inspired many of Grand Master Lu's followers, most of whom can likely read the original work in Chinese. This English translation not only makes it available to followers who are not fluent in Chinese, but also to the larger audience, of English speaking spiritual seekers and scholars around the world. It should be of great interest to students and scholars of comparative religion, being a new contribution to the genre of mystical literature. It is a great honor to have the privilege to read, and write the foreword to, this inspiring work.

David B. Gray
Associate Professor of Religious Studies
Santa Clara University
May 27, 2010
15th day of the 4th Lunar Month, Iron Tiger Year

In my spiritual travel, I performed mystical salvations. I arrived at an understanding of "faith, understanding, practice, and realization." I came to know what "silence" was.

Sheng-yen Lu

1 Travel to Worlds Beyond - Preface

While I was in retreat at Leaf Lake, I cut myself off from the rest of the world and gradually became less aware of what was happening outside. However, the frequency of my spiritual traveling had increased. I discovered that the mind worked in many ways. Within the ten directions, there were thousands and thousands of events happening in different shapes and forms that were just too numerous to talk and write about.

The book, *Crossing the Ocean of Life and Death* is a testimony to spiritual travel. I feel that it is an important book. It states that [life and death] is "the biggest event in life." Those who cultivate will know where to go after death, while those who don't will turn into illusive entities of ignorance, and drift within the cycle of birth and death.

During my years in retreat, I suffered many illnesses. I asked the Buddha, "Why did this happen?"

The Buddha replied, "It is natural."

"Why must there be the suffering of illness in life?"

"Because you are very close to the summit of the mountain."

Since it was natural for my body to have such ailments, I did not care much about it then. Instead, I focused more effort on spiritual traveling during my meditation. I discovered that the nature of the mind is limitless and boundless, and it is as wide as the ten directions. A lot of Buddhist theories could be proven and written through my spiritual travels.

Let me tell you about a mysterious incident. When I came down with the "splitting headache," it was the most excruciating moment in my life. My body could barely handle it and it caused me a great deal of anxiety.

However, I sat down quietly and forgot about my body and mind. The mysterious state of selflessness emerged and as a result, a buddha appeared, radiating three beams of light upon me. Immediately, I was filled with dharma bliss and all of my afflictions disappeared. This was the most natural, genuine, happy and efficient way of liberation.

In my spiritual travel, I performed mystical salvations. I arrived at an understanding of "faith, understanding, practice, and realization." I came to know what "silence" was.

This is my 166th book, which is about spiritual travels. As I write this, I am filled with joy and the flavor of dharma.

I feel that a life of spiritual traveling is not empty. It is in fact very meaningful.

May all who read this book receive great deliverance.

Sheng-yen Lu
17102 NE 40th CT.
Redmond, WA 98052
U.S.A.

2 The Grand Opening Ceremony

During one of my spiritual explorations, I saw a crowd of people. In fact, they weren't actually humans, or non-humans, but they were a group of evil spirits wandering in space. They proceeded in one direction and I followed behind them, concealing my three streams of auric radiance.

We arrived at a temple that appeared grand and resplendent. A sign at the top read "Divine Spirit of Prominence." Incidentally, it was the temple's grand opening.

All of the evil spirits entered, and I followed after them. During the grand opening ceremony, a monk was performing the "opening of the eyes" consecration for the statues, while laymen dressed in black full-sleeve robes were reciting sutras. There were an astonishing number of statues that were all bright and shining, that had been donated by the faithful followers. The entities began to speak.

One little ghost said, "I want to possess the body of the Third Crown Prince."

A female ghost remarked, "I want to be Guanyin Bodhisattva."

An old ghost exclaimed, "I want to be the Earth Deity."

A drunken ghost stated, "I want to be Living Buddha Ji Gong."

A yaksa spoke, "I want to be Cheng Huang, the City God."

……

Through my observation, I saw that there was no radiance around the monk whose aura was as filthy as mud as he was far from being a cultivator of substance. So how could he possibly attract any light into the statues in the absence of his own light? No wonder evil spirits were attracted and scrambling to possess the statues. This could not be good. The splendor of the temple, statues, and ceremony was really tarnished. As I was leaving, the spirit of an old fox stopped me.

He said, "Your aura is pure and pristine. You have spiritual powers and complete freedom. You are capable of ascending to the heaven and becoming an immortal. You have attained the union of San Yuan, the Three Originals, as in the heaven, earth and humanity. Hence you are free and unhindered. Yet why do you still go about on your spiritual journey? Wouldn't it be better for you to inhabit the statue of Shakyamuni Buddha and enjoy offerings from the humans? With your presence at the temple, negative energy would be cleansed, and the Three Poisons and Six Desires would be eradicated. All sentient beings would be saved. What do you think?"

I was appalled, "No, no, if I should dwell in the enjoyment of human offerings, then all of my previous efforts will be wasted. This is not what I want."

"If you aren't here for Shakyamuni Buddha, then why did you come here?"

"I'm just passing by on my spiritual journey."

"If you're only here to join in the celebration, then I will inhabit the statue." The old fox spirit then immediately possessed the statue of Shakyamuni Buddha.

I left the temple quietly, looking at the sky and sighed. So much for the grand consecration ceremony whose overly elaborate formalities were really a superficial display of no substance.

The monks involved in the ceremony today are only in a rush to perform repentance chanting. They lack the actual commitment in keeping the Five Precepts and the Ten Good Deeds and practicing the Six Perfections, and they develop little concentration stability and wisdom. It would be easy for contemporary monks to make a living this way.

Besides studying the repentance sutras in depth, one must truly understand the inner meanings of the sutras, practicing and validating the realization through one's example, to be considered as a true monk! (One must be well-versed in the Tripitaka, practice the Buddhadharma, and take the Dharma as one's teacher.)

I knew that if I inhabited Shakyamuni Buddha's statue, I would indeed have food, clothing, and shelter. People would respect me and give me offerings, and I would feel very blessed. However, I, the person at Leaf Lake would certainly die during my sitting meditation. Besides, I figured if I had inhabited Shakyamuni Buddha's statue, I would be impersonating the Buddha.

This brings to mind Monk Dushun of the Tang Dynasty who was the emanation of Manjushri Bodhisattva. Any time that he gazed at a temple occupied by pseudo deities or ghosts, be they tree-deities, evil dragons or other spirits, the temples would catch on fire. If I inhabited these statues and if Monk Dushun or any other high monks happened to come to the temple, then I would be doomed. The purpose of my practice isn't to ask for anything in return, but to exercise bodhicitta truthfully, with the real dedication of attaining buddhahood and saving sentient beings.

It was a good thing that my mind was clear and sound. Although I was traveling spiritually, my mind was absolutely clear and unambiguous, unperturbed by all the diverse views around me. It's crucial for me to understand how to apply absolute wisdom and right thought as I walk on the great path of the right dharma. When a person is free and able to let go, then why should he be worshipped by others and enjoy their offerings of incense?

As well, there were so many evil spirits in that temple. There were also countless pre-occupations with worldly matters, and too many problems requiring consultations and divinations, which all would never cease to end. Such countless worries and trivial matters would never be gone. I would only get entangled in the recurring cycle of cause and effect, and the six realms of existence.

All of this would happen to me if I impersonated Shakyamuni. My sweat dripped profusely and I immediately left the temple to continue on my spiritual journey.

Traveling in light is fast. Within a split second, I would be thousands of miles away. I heard the old fox spirit shouting from behind, "Sir, please stay for a few more days. Stay as a guest here. The ceremony will last for seven days. You can eat your heart out."

I gestured to him, thanked him, and then left.

As I continued in my spiritual journey, I suddenly saw sparks of fire everywhere as though there was a huge fire that was shining brightly. I looked carefully and the fire was coming from the beaks of some osprey-like crows, which had long claws and pitch black bodies with white bellies. I cried out in alarm! This was the Fire Crow Battalion.

Following behind the Fire Crow Battalion was a deity who was riding on a cloud chariot, driven by two dragons. He was none other than the fire god Zhu Rong.

"Where are you going?" I asked.

When the fire god, an old acquaintance of mine, saw me he told me right away, "There's a new temple down the hill. After the grand consecration ceremony, it was occupied by evil spirits. I'm going to take the Fire Crow Battalion to burn the temple and prevent it from becoming a future dwelling place for demons, which may cause harm to people." I was speechless but I quietly uttered to myself, "How lucky I am!"

There are traps everywhere for a practitioner. One needs to avoid desires as well as all evil ways. Even though I have the power of spiritual travel, my mind must be at ease and free in order to cleanse the Three Poisons. There is only one goal in the future and that is to return to the Maha Twin Lotus Ponds. The responsibility of a practitioner is to spread the dharma. This way, life can be beautiful. One must persevere and purify the mind continuously.

Nevertheless, I thought of a poem by Bai Juyi:

> **A pasture in the distant plain**
> **Withers as the years pass by**
> **No wildfire can destroy the grass**
> **It grows again when the spring winds blow**

There is only one goal in the future and that is to return to the Maha Twin Lotus Ponds. The responsibility of a practitioner is to spread the dharma. This way, life can be beautiful. One must persevere and purify the mind continuously.

Sheng-yen Lu

3 Infinite Transformations

In my spiritual journey, I visited Shakyamuni Buddha's dwelling place. During that time, I circumambulated the Buddha three times and afterwards, I sang this verse:

> **Homage to Shakyamuni Buddha**
> **The king of preachers in the Saha world**
> **With others, I take refuge in the Buddha**
> **The teacher of gods and men**

I said, "Oh Buddha! With your mighty power, I was able to arrive at your place. I have two questions, which are also asked by sentient beings. The first question is, 'Who am I?' The second question is, 'Oh Buddha! Where are you?'"

I could not describe the Buddha's dwelling place in words. I could only say, "Divine, clear, tranquil, permanent, luminous, and bright."

The Buddha heard my two questions. He smiled and answered, "Regarding the first question, let me ask you. 'Who exactly are you?'"

The Buddha continued, "Regarding the second question, you have always chanted the 'Pure Dharmakaya Buddha' praise. So let me ask you. 'Where exactly is the Buddha?'"

When I heard this, I was dumbfounded.

Was I asking the Buddha questions or was the Buddha asking me questions? However, I immediately understood what he meant though.

I replied, "The first question cannot be answered. I will do my own practice. The answer to the second question is: the buddhas of the ten directions and three times, and infinite transformations."

The Buddha heard my answers, nodded his head, and smiled.

Now let me tell everyone that all of the Zen (Chan) Patriarchs of China studied the first question:

Why did Bodhidharma come from the West?

What is your original face before you were born?

Who is reciting the Buddha's name?

All things belong to one, but where does one belong to?

What is the Buddha-nature?

There are also Yunmen's pastry, Zhaozhou's tea, Linji's shouting, Deshan's stick, Tianlong's finger, Jiashan's abode, Nanquan's cat, among others [note: these are stories of Chinese Chan masters, and they are known in Japanese Zen as Ummon, Joshu, Rinzai, Tokuzan Senkan, Tenryu, Kassan Zenne, and Nansen Fugan, respectively].

Now, let me ask you this:

"Who are you?"

Please study this.

As for the second question, "Oh Buddha! Where are you?" The Buddha represents the trikaya [three bodies] of the Tathagata. There is the dharmakaya truth body, the sambhogakaya bliss body, and the nirmanakaya emanation body. The dharmakaya is absolute, constant, and omnipresent. It unites with the wisdom of the practitioner leading to fine merits of the sambhogakaya, the body of bliss. Realizing this principle, and acting according to circumstances with superb, subtle, and infinite manifestations is the nirmanakaya emanation body.

Thus, the dharmakaya is the essence, sambhogakaya is the form, and nirmanakaya is the function. For example, Vairocana Buddha, can manifest innumerable emanation bodies. [While seated on a lotus pedestal and surrounded by a thousand flowers]; each flower supports a hundred million worlds, and within each world a Shakyamuni Buddha appears.

I asked people in turn, "Oh Buddha, where exactly are you?"

If you still can't figure it out, then let me point it out to you again.

The essence of the mind of all beings is absolute and equal, and there is non-birth, non-death, non-increasing, non-decreasing, and it is eternal. Observe yourself and purify your deluded mind to manifest your sambhogakaya and nirmanakaya to teach and convert other sentient beings to transcend to the nirvana of eternity, bliss, true self, and purity.

Vairocana Buddha (the Great Sun Tathagata) is the dharmakaya of Padmakumara, Amitabha Buddha is the sambhogakaya of Padmakumara, and Living Buddha Lian-sheng is the nirmanakaya of Padmakumara.

By transmitting the True Buddha Tantra, I want to pass on the words of truth and real evidence to my students.

I truly witnessed the Maha Twin Lotus Ponds of the Western Paradise of Ultimate Bliss. I absolutely am not fabricating stories. I did journey into the Great Void and met Maha White Padmakumara. I knew I was the nirmanakaya of Padmakumara. (This was mentioned in my book thirty or more years ago.)

Once you receive the lineage of Vairocana Buddha, Amitabha Buddha, Padmakumara and Living Buddha Lian-sheng, and resonate with them, you can achieve union, manifestation, and connection.

This can be expressed as:
>One moon is reflected in thousands of rivers.
>One sound expresses all dharmas.
>One mind transcends the buddha land.

Through the True Buddha Tantra, the body, speech, and mind are purified. You'll receive pure blessings and transformative power; your faith will carry you onwards, and the transformative effect is infinite.

I will give an example. After a group practice at one of the True Buddha chapters, a disciple stood up and said, "Last night I dreamt that our Grand Master in Seattle was giving something to me."

Before this disciple could finish, two other disciples stood up and said, "We also dreamt that our Grand Master was giving something to us."

At this moment, the chapter's leader said, "Let's do it this way! Don't reveal what Grand Master gave to you. Write your answer on a piece of paper and hand it to me, so that we can all find out together."

They each wrote it on a piece of paper and handed it to the chapter's leader. The leader opened all three papers and was shocked to find out that all three people had written the same thing: "longevity peach." When this was announced, everyone looked at each other. This happened because it was the birthday of Amitabha Buddha.

Let me say this:

A person only has to attain "one-pointedness" with his mind, and this one-pointedness is focusing the mind so that there are no distracting thoughts. Wholeheartedly think of Grand Master or chant his heart mantra, **OM GURU LIAN SHENG SIDDHI HUM**. When the mind no longer has wild and distracting thoughts, the mind will transcend the state of thought and anxiety.

You should know that when I am abiding in one-pointedness of mind, three thousand phenomena become integrated as one complete reality all at once. This is no difference from the contemplation method of the Tiantai School.

By having wholehearted faith in achieving union with Padmakumara, you shall achieve union. Within an instant, you will be able to see Padmakumara in your meditation or dream.

I can travel and manifest myself spiritually in many places. As long as practitioners start at the point of one-pointedness of mind, they can easily connect with Padmakumara, receive his empowerment, blessings, protection, increase their good fortune and wisdom, gain rebirth in the buddha land, and undoubtedly be able to go to any pure land.

This can be expressed as:
>Abiding in one-pointedness of mind without distraction.
>Abiding in one-pointedness of mind without delusion.
>Reciting the Buddha's name with one-pointedness.
>Reciting the mantra with one-pointedness.
>Devotion to the Buddha with one-pointedness.

A person only has to attain "one-pointedness" with his mind, and this one-pointedness is focusing the mind so that there are no distracting thoughts. Wholeheartedly think of Grand Master or chant his heart mantra, OM GURU LIAN SHENG SIDDHI HUM. When the mind no longer has wild and distracting thoughts, the mind will transcend the state of thought and anxiety.

Sheng-yen Lu

4 Rescuing a Person Committing Suicide

While traveling spiritually, I saw a man standing on top of a tall building, attempting to jump and kill himself. This kind of incident is a frequent occurrence nowadays.

This man was not old. There were people down below who noticed this unusual behavior, and called in a fire truck, ladder, and air cushion. The crowd was boisterously noisy.

Somebody approached this man and tried to talk him out of jumping. However, the man got more agitated and attempted to jump. Seeing this, the crowd screamed and the rescuer backed off.

While traveling spiritually in space, I saw that the man who wanted to jump was not alone. He was suffering from depression, an indication that his state of mind was influenced by dark forces. He was surrounded by fetus spirits (resulted from abortion), malicious entities (resulted from accidents and unnatural death), and begrudged spirits (karmic creditors).

The fetus spirits shouted, "You took our lives, so go to hell!"

The malicious entities shouted, "Death pays all debts. All sufferings shall vanish."

The begrudged spirits demanded, "Curse you to your death. Let us die together!"

Under the influence of the spirits, the man seemed very determined to die.

Suicide is the seed of suffering. There are many kinds of suffering in life. There are sufferings of birth, old age, illness, death, worries, hatred, torment, anxiety, mental afflictions, the cycle of life and death, and the retribution of debts from begrudged creditors. Suffering is endless.

The seed of suicide grows from the mind of humans. This suicidal thought then reverberates through space, which magnetizes many malicious spirits to one. These spirits are greedy, selfish, hateful, and ignorant, and they want you to kill yourself.

I realized why people such as Ernest Hemingway, Yasunari Kawabata, Yukio Mishima, and San Mao all killed themselves.

They were tired! To them, suffering seemed endless!

So despite their great fame and wealth, why did they commit suicide?

This is due to a shift in these people's state of minds. When they are unable to resolve their internal chaos, the thought of suicide arises, haunting them like demons.

Practitioners must pay attention to this kind of situation.

A person who is fixated in the White Skeleton Visualization may find life meaningless.

Overly engrossed in the Contemplation on Impurity one may become disinterested towards life.

Practitioners must watch out. Too much or too little of anything are not healthy.

Practitioners must know that a zealous mind surpasses kalpas of suffering in samsara. The world is a field of practice for those who have come here. There must be dharma bliss in order to ascend to the utmost joy of the nine grades of rebirth in Sukhavati, the Western Paradise of Ultimate Bliss.

Practice is the "golden jade."
Suicide is the "sandstone."
One must clearly understand the benefits of the Buddhist teachings that lead one to achieve dharma bliss, depart from suffering, and attain happiness. We must not be confused.

Suicide only brings suffering and not happiness. The act of suicide is tantamount to killing the buddha!

Spiritual practice requires one to be alive, and life hinges on the will to live. In order to live, one must live well. We all know life is hard. By sacrificing ourselves to practice, we will be in control of our survival, which depends only upon oneself, and not others, the environment or what other people think. A practitioner should therefore recognize these things:

> The value of his own life.
> The recognition of his Buddha-nature.
> Achieving freedom through letting go.
> Gaining happiness through freedom.

Always adding credit to the luminosity and color of your life.

I observed that man again and he really was going to jump. I was overwhelmed with compassion and wanted to save him, so I emitted the buddha light, spiritual light and white light onto him. When the fetus spirits, malicious entities, and begrudged spirits saw these lights, they were all frightened and ran away, disappearing in an instant.

The man suddenly came to his senses and I manifested a few scenes of death to show him the end results of jumping off the building. He couldn't bear to watch them.

Suddenly, he heard the voices of his parents, and he gave up and stopped what he was doing. Seizing the golden opportunity, the rescuer rushed towards him and saved him.

I thought of this poem while departing the scene:

Seeing someone attempting to jump from the building

**Where he stands only a hairline from danger
Even if one could own all the mountains and rivers
Transmitting the Buddhadharma with equanimity is all that matters**

登寶佛教文物流通
True Buddha Temple Maryland Bookstore
1930 Spencerville Road, Spencerville, MD 20868 U.S.A.
Tel: (301) 421-9298

收 據 (Receipt)

日期 Date: 9-29-11

Invoice #: 005287

英文姓名 English Name: _____

地址 Street Address: _____

City: _____ State: _____ Zip Code: _____

電話 Office Phone: _____ Home Phone: _____

Item #	Description	Qty.	Price	Amount
	Candles			5 —
	Incense			20 —
	Book			9 —
			Sub-Total	
			Tax	
Cash ___X___ Check # _____			Freight	
Credit Card : **American Express, Discover, MasterCard, Visa**			Total	34 —
Received By: _____cc_____			Deposit	
Customer Signature: _____			Balance	

No Refund No Exchange

5 A Sad Love Song

I once heard a young lady praying, "**OM GURU LIAN SHENG SIDDHI HUM**. Grand Master, Living Buddha Lian-sheng, Sheng-yen Lu, I have done fire offerings [or homas] forty-nine times. I shall now call upon Kurukulla to bless me with love and harmony. Act now in accordance to your vow, and grant me my wish to marry my male friend."

She was praying very sincerely, "Please Grand Master! Please Kurukulla!"

The fire offering of Vajrayana Buddhism is very powerful. That was why I could clearly hear her vigorous plea when I was journeying spiritually.

Answering her prayer, I went to find out about her male friend. I was surprised to find out the man in question was also my student. So, it turned out that a female student of mine was in love with one of my male students. She was madly in love with him.

She would often wait at the front door of his house after he returned home from work, just to say hello and chat with him. However, the man would always avoid her whenever possible.

What astonished me even more was that he too was making fire offerings. His homas involved Ragaraja. He also prayed sincerely, "**OM GURU LIAN SHENG SIDDHI HUM**. Grand Master, Living Buddha Lian-sheng Sheng-ye Lu, I have done the Ragaraja fire offering forty-nine times. Please empower me and my girlfriend so that we can get married."

The problem was that while the girl was madly infatuated with the man, the man was actually in love with another woman, and not this girl.

One day the man took his girlfriend home in his Mercedes-Benz. They were very intimate, holding hands, and kissing each other. When the other girl saw this, she was dumbfounded. Saddened, she watched silently as he put his arm around his girlfriend's waist and entered the house with her, shutting the door behind them.

Extremely depressed, she could no longer hold back her tears. She had waited for him to return home, only to witness that scene.

She wasn't discouraged though, and returned home to pray and did a homa again, repeatedly crying out loudly, "**OM GURU LIAN SHENG SIDDHI HUM**. Grand Master, don't you hear me?"

"Namo Kurukulla. I will marry no one but him and he will marry no one but me. Do you hear that?"

The fire burned ever so intensely. Yet, this man remained madly in love with his present girlfriend and he had absolutely no feelings for my female student despite her homas.

He also very diligently cultivated the Ragaraja Practice and chanted the Ragaraja Mantra countless times and knew it by heart.

As a result, I met up with Kurukulla and Ragaraja and we discussed these two disciples doing homas and their wishes.

We looked at four major issues:

1. The cause and effect of love between the three of them.
2. What results would be seen as fair and equal for all parties?
3. Will their faith [in Buddhism] be increased through the

power of fire offering?
4. Could we prevent all of them from being hurt?

The outcome of the meeting was:
Kurukulla shook her head.
Ragaraja shook his head.
I shook my head.

The entanglement of affection and love never ends as it cannot be resolved. Those who are obsessed with such self-induced love will surely suffer mental anguish and agony. Those who are obsessed with such love are possessive, and are forever trapped in a never-ending cycle, for they are thrilled when things go their way but become infuriated when things don't go their way. The solution to this issue is simply to let things take their natural course.

I still felt sorry for my female student though. I knew her prayer would not be answered. Even if she did hundreds of fire offerings, Kurukulla could not help her. Even I could not help her.

I spoke into her ear, "My student, you beg me for help, but who do I turn to?"

She heard my voice but couldn't see me. She looked around puzzled and couldn't understand me. The only thing I could do was to continue on in my spiritual journey.

All love arises from causes and conditions. Some affinities are deep, while others are weak. Some affinities will ripen, while others will not. People can make fire offerings and pray, and though they would receive blessings, it would be very hard to change things if the karma and conditions are already fixed.

When all conditions are complete, then cause and affinity shall ripen. If conditions are not met, then nothing shall result even if you insist.

I'm not saying that Vajrayana practices have no power. I'm saying that attachment to the ego, egotistical views, satkayadrsti [the false belief in a permanent individuality], strong desires, materialistic forms and fixed karma are all very difficult to transform.

I have tried my best to awaken this disciple and hope she would let go, which is the only way to stop her mental afflictions.

The man eventually got married. She was not the bride.

Anger is a very dreadful thing in humans. Once her anger arose from deep within, she would be mad at the man and his bride, and her anger and hatred might even spill over to her parents, siblings and everyone else.

Anger can change everything. Eventually she would completely lose her morals, ethics, wisdom, religious beliefs, and tolerance as her heart would be forever consumed by hatred and dissatisfaction. It would be impossible for her to be happy and experience the joy of tranquility.

She couldn't maintain emotional balance anymore. She hated Grand Master for not granting her an answer. She hated homas and hated Kurukulla for not helping her.

She got rid of her picture of Grand Master and all the buddha statues on her shrine, and gave away her fire offering stove. She threw away all of her implements and burned her robe. Hatred! Hatred! Hatred! Her hatred lingered without end.

I cried in vain, as I could not change her mind. She tore up her refuge certificate.

I felt ashamed that I couldn't help her. I blamed myself and I was ashamed of myself that I wasn't able to help her. I was sad but I couldn't do anything about her situation.

Sentient beings have desires and many of them take refuge in order to satisfy their desires. In fact, once a person has taken refuge, the individual must contemplate upon the ways of causes and conditions. Those who constantly dwell on desires may, in fact, easily lose their confidence in the dharma.

Ponder this:

> You take nothing with you upon death.
> Only your karma shall follow.
> When desires are not satisfied,
> Your Buddhist practice deteriorates to the dark side.

Once you take refuge, you must develop bodhicitta, pursue buddhahood, and help sentient beings. This is achieved without asking for anything in return and by realizing the "Emptiness of the Three Wheels" [attaining emptiness of the giver, the receiver, and the gift when giving to others] and practice non-attachment. The bodhicitta that is then generated will not cause any harm to others and oneself. A true Buddhist is one who is free of concerns, free from the defiled mind, free from hindrances, free from anxieties, free from mental afflictions, and free from worries.

When we make a fire offering, we request the buddhas and bodhisattvas to bless us as much as possible. At the same time however, we must be aware of all superficial appearances in the world, whether it is success or failure, prosperity or poverty, are in fact momentary phenomena. What we know as "formation, duration, deterioration, and extinction," "arising, duration, change, and extinction," "impermanence," "egolessness," "suffering" and "emptiness" are the results of causes and conditions (love and romance arise from affinity).

When practicing Buddhism, we should aim to achieve kindness, purity, illumination, and finally, liberation.

We practice Buddhism to learn the wisdom of liberation and the wisdom of bodhi. Practitioners should be filled with dharma joy, a sense of contentment which brings constant delight that attracts health and joy, allowing us to see the beauty in all things, and be grateful for everything in life. Practitioners should spread the joy of the dharma just like the incense smoke that permeates in the air, touching all sentient beings.

A blessed life is attained when greed, anger, and ignorance are eliminated. This is the true view of life. Jealousy and hatred are not right views. Buddhist practitioners must understand that Buddhism is established on the right view that cause and effect do exist. When you hate someone or something, you are the first to suffer from your own anger.

To those who have taken refuge, I want to say this to you. Do you know Grand Master's heart? Upon taking refuge, your heart must be in oneness with mine. Do you know my vows? Upon taking refuge, you must abide by these vows. Do you know the teachings of my True Buddha Tantra? Upon taking refuge, you must understand these dharma teachings. Do not let romantic feelings run your life.

I hope those who practice homas (the fire offerings) will focus their minds single-pointedly on making offerings, doing charity, persevering, chanting mantras, being thankful and taking refuge, instead of praying, praying, and praying. How can praying ever satisfy anyone?

6 Ghost Feasts

Once I met a Ghost King who was also traveling, so I accompanied him and we both traveled together.

I asked the Ghost King, "Someone asked the Buddha about making offerings to spirits. The Buddha replied that one doesn't need to do that, but if someone wants to perform offering rituals, one may initiate them as one wishes. What do you think?"

The Ghost King answered, "The Buddha meant that it is really about the heart, and not measured by the superficial display of the deliverance ritual."

I asked again, "Will the spirit world receive the offerings?"

The Ghost King replied, "Buddhas, bodhisattva, pratyekabuddhas, and sravakas are spiritual beings of the four holy realms, and all offerings are received as a gesture of the heart. The heavenly realm is a blissful world and making offerings to the heavens is really an expression of gratitude. In general ritual offerings are not made to living beings in the human world. The animal world exists as a karmic consequence of ignorance. Hence, they are also unable to receive any ritual offerings. In the hell realm, beings suffer the most. Therefore, ritual offerings offer little benefit unless they are performed by high monks such as Maudgalyayana and others. As far as I know, only ghosts and godly spirits are able to receive the offerings. In fact, these spirits are looking to humans for these offerings."

"Do you mean that they really could consume the food and see the flowers?"

The Ghost King answered, "Yes, spirits consume food by touch and they can see everything."

The Ghost King added, "Men have to sleep to replenish their energy. They consume food to maintain their bodies. All spirits eat by touch."

"What exactly is food consumption by touch?" I asked.

The Ghost King laughed, "Animals bite animals. One subjugates the other and animals eat each other. This is touch. Humans eat rice and flour. This is touch. As for spirits, they do the same through touch. These beings are not exactly in the high spiritual realm."

I asked, "You mean the act of eating can be differentiated?"

The Ghost King explained, "Those in the high spiritual realms consume by partaking in thought, consciousness and the joy of samadhi. Those in the lower spiritual realms, such as animals, bite each other for the flesh. Those in the ghost realm drink blood for food. Those in the hell realm consume fire. Humans are not high on the spiritual scale either."

The Ghost King continued, "Actually, in the ghost realm the spirits consume many things. Some feed on qi or subtle energy, some settle for water, some feed on aroma, some get energized through sleep, some zap the vital energy of people. These are considered healthy. Others feed on feces, urine, blood, meat, menstrual blood and even poisons."

I was shocked.

The Ghost King remarked, "You have seen it all. What is there to be afraid of? Men eat by touch too and they also eat indiscriminately. These days, there are also people who drink urine and stuff themselves with toxic food."

I nodded.

I asked, "What do you think is the most important thing when giving offerings to spirits?"

The Ghost King replied, "The most important thing is intention. It needs to be practical. Cooked food represents good intention. One or two types of food are good enough. Quantity is not the problem. The person who performs the ritual of offering must know how to transform his intention. This is how mandala offerings are made in Vajrayana Buddhism."

"Why must it be cooked food?" I asked.

"Many ghosts like cooked food, and not canned food because cooked food is done with the heart."

"What is the Meng Shan Food Offering Ritual?"

The Ghost King replied, "This is the method used to deliver the hungry ghosts. Meng Shan or Meng Mountain is the name of a place. There was a high monk named Ganlu, who devised this method to deliver the hungry ghosts, which resulted in the Ritual of the Meng Shan Food Offering."

"What is the Yogacara Flaming Mouth?"

"It is a food offering ritual in Vajrayana Buddhism that has been empowered by the buddhas. It is very powerful."

"What else is there beside food offering?"

"Dharma offering simply means to offer someone Dharma. One example of this is the Precious Emperor Liang Repentance which came about due to the empress's extreme jealousy. She killed a concubine with poisonous tea and even became jealous when the emperor was too close to his Zen (Chan) master, Master Zhigong. After the empress died, she was reborn as a python. Her body was ridden with poisonous worms that bit her continuously under her scales. It was extremely painful."

The Ghost King continued, "Later when the emperor was thinking about the empress, the python appeared in the forbidden garden. Its body smelled like filth causing the emperor to turn away and leave. Just at that moment though, the python began to speak in a human voice. The empress said that due to her jealousy, she was reborn in the form of a python. She begged the emperor to perform deliverance for her to release her suffering. So, the emperor gathered all of the monks to perform a repentance ritual. Zen Master Zhigong gathered all the repentance practice texts and compiled them into one great repentance practice. With the blessing power invoked through the names of the respective buddhas, he gathered five hundred monks and performed the repentance ritual for her. During the repentance ceremony, the python coiled around a pillar and listened to the discourse. When the repentance ceremony was over, the palace was filled with heavenly fragrance and music. The empress rose to the Trayastrimsa Heaven and became a heavenly being. This was the power of the Precious Emperor Liang Repentance which is an example of dharma offering."

I asked, "Is dharma offering more important than food offering?"

The Ghost King answered, "Food offering only satisfies hunger for awhile. Dharma offering can elevate one to heaven and therefore, it ranks first."

"Is there a particular time to do the food offering?"

The Ghost King explained, "Offerings to the buddhas are done at noon. As for the devas, it is performed at dawn. For ghosts, it is done at night and for the elementals, it is carried out in the evening. This is called the 'Four Meal Times.'"

I commented, "There aren't any specific times when I make my offerings. I just do it when there is food."

The Ghost King remarked, "You are Living Buddha Lian-sheng, Sheng-yen Lu. When you manifest your intention, then that would be the time you do your offerings. All the buddhas, bodhisattvas, vajra protectors, heavenly beings and ghost spirits will be present when you make your offerings. You are the Great Vajra Vidyadhara Acharya and therefore, you are different from others."

I thought about some other questions, "What about burning paper money?"

The Ghost King laughed, "It's the same as burning incense."

"How is it the same?"

"It's all in the heart."

"What aspect of the heart?"

The Ghost King answered, "The filial heart, the thankful heart, the respectful heart, the sincere heart, the heart of dedication, and the heart of deliverance. Each expression involves the heart."

"What thoughts go into deliverance?"

"By invoking the empowerment of the buddhas for the purification of the body, speech, and mind in order to achieve deliverance, so that the dead can attain rebirth in the buddha land."

"Is that possible?"

"Do it sincerely."

I raised these questions as I traveled with the Ghost King.

During the entire time, I was the one bringing up the questions.

Suddenly, the Ghost King asked me, "Living Buddha Lian-sheng, let me ask you something instead. One step forward is death and one step backward is death. If you can't move forward or backward, it is liken to being drown in this pool of dead water. What would you do to get out of this predicament?"

I answered, "A verse in *The Avatamsaka Sutra* states:

**If you wish to know
All buddhas of three times
You should observe the nature of the dharma realm
And see that all is created by the mind**"

The Ghost King nodded and asked, "If there is a tiger in front of you, a wolf behind you, a deep swamp on your left and a cliff on your right, what would you do to resolve this?"

I answered:

> **Neither falling into existence nor non-existence**
> **Leaving both sentiment and explanation**
> **Past, present and future are one reality**
> **Omnipresence**

Upon hearing that, the Ghost King instantly soared into the sky and disappeared. Appearing in space was an adamantine jeweled land, adorned with exquisite jewel discs and pure clear crystals. A jeweled canopy adorned with exquisitely scented necklace of precious stones was constantly emitting shining light, and producing beautiful sound. Below the jeweled canopy was a bodhisattva with an adamantine body clothed in a garment made of lapis lazuli, and was seated on a great white elephant. His entire body was emitting rays of illumination.

I closed my palms sincerely and spoke, "Samantabhadra Bodhisattva!"

"Yes."

"You transformed into the Ghost King to help sentient beings!"

"My transformations are endless. Through the approach of question and answer, I am able to give a myriad of teachings."

It did cross my mind that this Ghost King, who seemed to know everything, was more than just a minor ghost king. He had to be the emanation of a great bodhisattva with extraordinary spiritual power.

I paid respect to Samantabhadra Bodhisattva.

Samantabhadra Bodhisattva said, "May you, Living Buddha Liansheng, continue to expound the vast perspective of enlightenment and that your subtle tones extending afar, there being no place they do not reach."

7 Don't Forget Your Vows

I met a dakini who was carrying fresh flowers, waiting to receive me in mid-air. When I looked closely, I recognized her. This dakini was one of my disciples. When she was alive, she helped me to deliver sentient beings so she quickly became a heavenly being.

I was surprised and questioned her, "You're dead?!"

The dakini cried and said, "Yes."

"How did you die?" I asked sadly.

"I was relatively OK the day before and I went for my rehabilitation exercise in the evening. However, during the night I just passed away."

My tears rolled uncontrollably. She was my good disciple!

I asked, "Where are you heading?"

She said, "When I was alive, I managed my own business so everyone was caught off guard when I departed. I came to see Grand Master today because I wanted to return to samsara to help with my business. I want to be reborn into the same family again and help them out with the business."

"I think this is really ridiculous. What belongs in samsara stays in samsara. Death pays all debts. You will be a laughingstock if you choose to incarnate [for business reason]."

"But business is important to me."

I stopped her, "Go back to the Maha Twin Lotus Ponds. If you incarnate into the human world, it will not be easy for you to return to the Pure Land."

"I don't want to go back to the Pure Land," the dakini uttered. She insisted on returning to the human world.

"Have you forgotten your vows?"

"What vows did I make to Grand Master?"

I showed her a scene:

Previously, she resided in the Maha Twin Lotus Ponds. According to the vows, when I (Living Buddha Lian-sheng) was about to incarnate into this world, I invited her to come along to help me. At first, she did not want to come due to the extreme suffering found in samsara's "Five Kasaya Periods of Chaos."

Hence:

A weak rhinoceros hangs onto the coral branch
The waves of the sea of suffering never end

I spoke:

While it is good to stay in the land of bliss
Sages and ordinary people are separated only by a thin line

It took a lot of effort before I could convince her to enter samsara. She was born first and I was born after her, so where age is concerned, she was a few years older than me.

I promised her this:

Amitabha Buddha is always within you
Once a defiled thought arises it separates you miles apart
There will be moments when you reflect

Do not forget your vows and pursue outer prosperity

I also promised her this:

**Just one trip to samsara before returning to the Pure Land
When you return you are still Guanyin**

These were my vows with the dakini but now, she had completely forgotten about them. She only wanted to return to the human world to start her business again.

During my retreat at Leaf Lake, I realized that the path on earth is difficult to tread. There are too many traps and entanglements, and too many hardships in the world. The chances of encountering the Buddhadharma are very slim, and even if one were to encounter the Buddhadharma, one may not necessarily believe and understand it, let alone practice and attain realization.

O Dakini! So you want to return to the human world to restart your business. Don't you know what suffering, emptiness, and impermanence are? Will the environment not change you? Will the environment not influence you? Will the environment not confuse you?

O Dakini! You took refuge in me in your lifetime and I recognized you. You also told me, "It was you who wanted me to descend into the world to help True Buddha School." I am here at Leaf Lake. Why do you want to return to the human realm again?

O Dakini!
Can you remain pure and happy?
Can you keep your spiritual conviction and not forget it?
Can you leave suffering and gain joy?
Can you purify your mind?
Can you return to the Maha Twin Lotus Ponds?

The real achievement for a person is the purification of the mind. Fame and fortune are insignificant. The greatest achievement is to rescue sentient beings from the wheel of suffering. With such a pure and unstained mind, the six realms of transmigration will be avoided. O Dakini! Do you have confidence and assurance of this when you return to earth?

Upon saying this, tears rolled down from her eyes. Her body trembled. I knew she did not have the confidence that she could return to the heavens again. This was my concern.

The dakini uttered, "Grand Master! What should I do?"

Her heart was struggling and she was in dilemma.

I told her again, "When human beings are too indulged in themselves, they are trapped in the ocean of suffering, much like living in a house that is on fire. All worldly beings suffer from torments. Everyone can agree that there is far more suffering than happiness. Though humans find themselves in the ocean of suffering, how many of them are truly able to see this illusion and let go? They are living in a dream that they cannot wake up from."

I added, "The Western Buddha Land of Ultimate Bliss emits voices of fine Dharma. The gem water flows and fills the lotus land, and the Tathagata and all sages there look impeccable. Pearls of good fortune glow with golden light amidst towers filled with treasures, and floors covered with golden sands. This is where you should go. You know that worldly affairs are like a dream but yet you still seek these dreams. You know about the risk of falling into the three realms of suffering, but you are still confused about where you should go? Have you not woken up from your dream yet?

The dakini replied, "What about my sons and grand children?"

I laughed, "They have their own destiny. Don't be enslaved by your attachment for them."

The dakini asked, "How do I go to the Western Paradise?"

I spoke this verse:

Once you release your burden, you will not feel the weight

**Lotus flowers will naturally blossom beneath your feet
If you chant the Buddha's name wholeheartedly
There is no need to pre-arrange the lotus seat**

The dakini recited, "Namo thirty-six trillion, one hundred nineteen thousand, and five hundred Amitabha Buddhas."

I immediately transformed from the image of Grand Master, Living Buddha Lian-sheng, Sheng-yen Lu into Amitabha Buddha of Boundless Life, appearing with the thirty-two marks, whose presence adorns the entire dharma realm. Lights emitted from the clouds around my body and I was holding a lotus seat. Everything was complete and sublime. When I released the lotus seat, the dakini stepped onto it.

The dakini questioned, "What exactly transpires during my chanting of the Buddha name?"

"There are ten kinds of mindfulness: dispassionate, serene mindfulness; pure, clear mindfulness; unmuddled mindfulness; thoroughly lucid mindfulness; mindfulness apart from defilement; mindfulness apart from various defilements; untainted mindfulness; radiant mindfulness; pleasant mindfulness; unhindered mindfulness. The chant that you just recited encompassed all these mindfulness."

"How do I leave now?"

"A single-pointed mind will take you there. You will be reborn instantaneously."

Within an instant the dakini appeared in the Maha Twin Lotus Ponds and was reborn in a lotus.

Once you release your burden, you will not feel the weight
Lotus flowers will naturally blossom beneath your feet
If you chant the Buddha's name wholeheartedly
There is no need to pre-arrange the lotus seat

            Sheng-yen Lu

8 My Impression on the Welcoming of the Buddha's Finger Relic

In my spiritual travel, I came across a blessing ceremony held for the welcoming of the Buddha's finger relic. The country's president, the respective governors and mayors, Buddhist elders, high monks, living buddhas and numerous followers all came to pay homage to the Buddha's finger relic.

Girls with draped hair allowed the possession of the Buddha's finger relic to tread on their hair. Others removed their garments and scattered flowers, so these would be stepped upon. There were those who bowed many times before the Buddha's finger relic.

It was a grand event for the world, the country, the society, the religion and all of its followers.

The Buddha's finger relic was paraded on a circuit with continuous crowds of people paying homage to it. I was moved to see so many people paying respect to the relic of Shakyamuni Buddha.

At the same time, I also saw people arguing over the authenticity of this Buddha's finger relic.

It reminded me of one incident during the Tang Dynasty when the Vinaya Master Daoxuan was walking at Xi Ming Monastery during the night. On his walk, he tripped on some steps and at that moment somebody suddenly caught a hold of him, preventing him from injury. When he got back up on his feet, he saw that the person who saved him was a young man.

Daoxuan asked, "Who are you? What are you doing here in the middle of the night?" The young man replied, "I am none other than Prince Nezha, the third son of Vaisravana. I have been your protector from a long time ago!"

Daoxuan remarked, "As far as my practice goes, I would never dare to bother you, the Third Prince, for no reason. Your mighty prince, is there any special Buddhist matter in India?"

The prince answered, "I have kept the Buddha's tooth relic with me for a long time. I would like to give it to you."

(It is a well known fact in the Buddhist circle that the tooth relic of Shakyamuni Buddha was presented to Vinaya Master Daoxuan by the Third Prince Nezha. Daoxuan was the religious head of the Southern Mountain Vinaya School. The precepts were among the three practices of the Tripitaka that were adopted by all schools. Daoxuan propagated the Four Part Vinaya (Dharmagupta Vinaya) of the Five Versions of the Vinaya. The Four Part Vinaya is the basis of the Vinaya or Precept School.)

Some people criticized that the tooth relic of Shakyamuni Buddha belonging to Vinaya Master Daoxuan was fake. After all, it was doubtful if the event that the Buddha's tooth relic was actually presented to Vinaya Master Daoxuan by Prince Nezha was fact and not fiction.

However, in my opinion, people should not criticize Vinaya Master Daoxuan for this reason:

After the Buddha had entered into nirvana, the precepts were widely taught by this master during the period of the semblance dharma.

(Vinaya Master Daoxuan observed the precepts very strictly. He always wore the three prescribed garments, had one meal a day, walked with a staff or cane, sat upright, and remained unperturbed by the fleas and worms that moved around him.)

In the past someone asked me, "Regarding the Buddha's relics, the Buddha's tooth relic, and the Buddha's finger relic, which ones are real? Which ones are fake?"

I replied, "Take Vinaya Master Daoxuan for example. If you believe his story then you would believe it. Otherwise, you won't. To believe or not to believe depends on the individual. The passing of the Buddha happened twenty-six hundred years ago, so how can we possibly authenticate anything? For example, Buddhists cannot pinpoint the exact birth date of Shakyamuni Buddha. Furthermore, the depictions of the Buddha's image were all based on imaginations, except for one illustration by the Buddha's disciple, Purna. However, it doesn't matter whether the relics are real or fake. I personally think that the Buddha's relics, his tooth relic, and his finger relic are worthy of our remembrance. The most important thing is the teachings of the Buddha which has true value in our life!"

I said:

It is useless just to talk about real or fake without taking refuge and obeying the precepts. Without the precepts, one cannot accumulate merit and become a buddha.

It is useless just to talk about real or fake without listening to the discourses. Without listening to the discourses, how can one practice and become a buddha.

It is useless just to talk about real or fake without purifying the body, speech, and mind. Without purifying yourself, you cannot become a buddha even if you bow until you bash your head.

We keep the precepts in order to conquer greed, practice meditation to conquer anger, and apply wisdom to conquer ignorance. (Cultivate diligently on the precepts, meditative stability, and wisdom so that we can eliminate greed, anger, and ignorance.)

People that keep the precepts must do so consistently. Those who recite the Buddha's name and mantra must constantly chant with a pure mind. In practicing meditative stability and cultivating wisdom, the heart shall flow in harmony with nature, and only then can the Buddha-nature manifest itself. By practicing the path to liberation or the path to enlightenment, we shall gain self-mastery over birth and death, and attain self-realization. This is more important than welcoming and paying homage to the Buddha's finger relic.

I have no objection towards welcoming the Buddha's relics, tooth relic and finger relic, neither do I object to the act of holding blessing ceremonies for the country, society and sentient beings. I also don't object to people prostrating before the Buddha's finger relic.

I only want Buddhist followers to remember that actual practice and the realization of our Buddha-nature is far more important than superficial worship.

Someone asked me, "What do you think about Han Yu's article 'Petition on the Buddha's Relics'?"

During my school days, this article was widely read. Han Yu was a famous writer and this article was one of his famous works. Han Yu advised Emperor Li Chun not to receive the Buddha's relics. These were his main points:

1. Buddhism was introduced into China during the time of Eastern Han Dynasty. Prior to that, Buddhism did not exist in China.
2. Prior to the arrival of Buddhism in China, each emperor had a long reign and there was peace and happiness. These emperors included the Yellow Emperor, Shaohao, Zhuanxu, Emperor Ku, Emperor Yao, Emperor Shun, Emperor Yu, Shangtang, Wuding, Emperor Zhou Wen, Emperor Zhou Wu and Emperor Zhou Mu, for example. These emperors remained in power for a long time. The longest reign lasted about a hundred years. Only Wuding's reign lasted for a mere fifty-nine years. Also, the lives of these emperors were very long and

many of them lived over a hundred years. The one with the shortest lifespan was Emperor Zhou Wu who lived up to the age of ninety-three. The citizens also lived very well.
3. Buddhism was introduced into China during the reign of Emperor Ming of the Eastern Han Dynasty. Following its introduction, Emperor Ming's reign only lasted for eighteen years. The emperors of the Southern and Northern Dynasties also believed in Buddhism. Their reigns were not long either and their lives were also short. There was continuous fighting and turmoil amongst the people. The world was not at peace.
(Only Emperor Wu of the Liang Dynasty had the longest reign of forty-eight years. He lived over eighty years old and was an enthusiastic believer in Buddhism. He even attempted to make an offering of himself to the Buddha three times. His later years were not good, however. A general by the name of Hou Jing rebelled against him and as a result, the emperor was surrounded and died of starvation inside the fortified city. Eight years later, the country also perished.)
4. Emperor Tang Gaozu, Li Yuan gave the order to eliminate the order of monks and nuns.
5. Confucius said, "Respect the ghost spirits and deities from a distance."
6. Han Yu suggested that Emperor Li Chun handled the Buddha's relics by "burning them in fire and dumping the ashes into water to end their existence forever. That would end everyone's doubts and problems for all future generations."

Regarding his [Han Yu] main points, I would like to clarify the following:

1. Before the Eastern Han Dynasty, Buddhism did not exist in China (there is no need to clarify this).

2. Prior to Buddhism being introduced into China, from the time of the Yellow Emperor to Emperor Zhou Mu, who were they exactly? Little did men know that these emperors were actually demigods. As far as I know, the Divine Sovereigns of the Three Origins, Three Grades and Three Officials were Yao, Shun, and Yu, who each lived a very long life and held reigns for a very long term, along with other emperors, for obvious reasons. Under the governance of these great gods, people lived peacefully. In ancient times, the hearts of men were pure and they had few desires. The world was naturally peaceful.
3. Subsequent emperors, however, had lots of desires and indulgences. Their behaviors were absurd. There were also many wars. As the saying goes, "the heart was not what it used to be," and these emperors were contaminated in their minds and no longer moderate their desires. Therefore, their reigns were shortened, along with their lifespan as well. These emperors were all just mundane beings, who were clearly no great deities. Thus, people naturally suffered. (Zen Master Zhigong had earlier revealed the karmic reasons surrounding the death of Emperor Wu of the Liang Dynasty by starvation in the fortress, which I shall not repeat here.)
4. Emperor Tang Gaozong, Li Yuan who eliminated the order of monks and nuns, was not the only emperor who committed this act. Throughout the history of China, Dharma crisis of Buddhism such as those carried out by the "Three Emperors of Wu and Emperor Zhou Shi Zong" were recorded. So long as emperors followed other religions, Buddhism would be persecuted and suppressed, monasteries would be destroyed, and the order of monks and nuns would be dissolved. There were many such cases of Dharma crisis.

I stated, "Buddhism had virtually become extinct in India, but what happened in India afterwards? It is the same thing.

The country was neither affluent nor peaceful. Buddhism was exterminated in Afghanistan. Even cultural heritage such as the two monumental standing Buddha statues of Bamyan was destroyed there. What can you say about the state of affair in Afghanistan since the incident? It is still no better.

5. Confucius said, "Respect the ghosts and deities, but keep a distance." The example cited by Han Yu was not logical. First, the Buddha's relics are not some ghosts or spirits. The Buddha is not a ghost or deity. Buddhism is not some superstitious worship of ghosts and spirits. The Buddha is an enlightened individual, a great sage who attained perfect self-realization and was willing to help others to attain realization, whose enlightenment and practice are complete and perfect.

    The teachings of the Buddha are concerned with "secular" and "profound" truths. They were not superstitious teachings about ghosts and spirits. The Buddha advocated compassion and equality. The Buddha's teachings are as vast as the ocean, not some teachings based on beliefs about spirits. The wisdom of the Buddha is Annutara-samyak-sambodhi, the unexcelled complete enlightenment. He has the Wisdom of the Seeds of Omniscience, which is prajna.

6. "Burning the relics in fire and dumping the ashes into water to end their existence forever. That would end everyone's doubts and problems for all future generations." To me, the Buddha's relics are a form of remembrance. Paying respect and giving thanks is alright. Burning them and throwing the ashes into water would be liken to making a mountain out of a mold. What doubts can arise when believing in the Buddha? What problems can arise when believing in the Buddha?

    Have you heard the saying of the book, *Tractate of the Most High One on Actions and Consequences*, which states, "Disasters and blessings have no entry gates of their own; they are invited by people."

In this Saha world, the profound knowledge and deep insight of the Buddha penetrate the truth of all things. If human beings do not practice the Buddha's teachings on the path to liberation and path to enlightenment, even if they live up to a hundred years, I don't see the meaning of their longevity.

In my spiritual travel, I was moved when I saw people paying sincere homage to the Buddha's relics. There were some who paid homage until midnight and continued from midnight until morning. Even when the temple had shut its doors, they still continued to pay homage towards the temple's doors. I even saw ghosts and deities coming to pay homage. Some truly came to pay homage while others came to mingle. They were even shouting and quarreling. When I took a closer look, I discovered that they were fighting over the names on plaques, and fighting for offerings and food. During the consecration of the Buddha's finger relic, there were lots of offerings such as incense, flowers, light, tea, fruits, and various others. The spirits fought over them.

I lamented at the sight. I saw the presence of an ancient immortal and asked, "Where is Han Yu now?"

The ancient immortal replied, "I think he is still in Chaozhou."

"So much history has passed by. Why is he still in Chaozhou?"

The ancient immortal explained, "During that year, when Emperor Li Chun read the petition on the Buddha's relics, he was furious and wanted to sentence Han Yu to death. Luckily the ministers Pei Du, Cui Qun, and others saved him. He was demoted to the position of a local administrator and sent to Chaozhou, Guangdong Province, located far away at the border. He remained frustrated until his death. Han Yu was a person fixated on blind loyalty. If the emperor never asked him to return, then he would stay in that place, and linger there even in death."

"For that long?"

"One thought pervades three thousand worlds. Time goes by quickly, and thousands of years are but an instant."

"How can people be saved?"

The ancient immortal uttered, "If people want to be liberated and wish to attain enlightenment [bodhi], I feel these three criteria must be met."

"What are these three criteria?"

"First, one must have the affinity to encounter a great spiritual teacher. Second, one's objective must be to attain the liberation from the cycle of life and death. Third, all worldly fame and gains must be relinquished. Only then can one be considered as a true Buddhist practitioner."

"May I know who this great spiritual teacher might be?" I asked.

The ancient immortal laughed, "Seemingly illusive, yet he is right before my eyes."

In my spiritual travel, I was moved when I saw people paying sincere homage to the Buddha's relics. There were some who paid homage until midnight and continued from midnight until morning.

Sheng-yen Lu

9 Half-Dead Samadhi

At the beginning of this book, the first few chapters speak of my spiritual travels. Spiritual travel itself is indeed marvelous. I call it "Half-Dead Samadhi."

The way I see it:

    Total death is true nirvana. The body is dead.

    Minor death is sleeping (deep unconscious sleep).

    Half-death is spiritual travel.

I have come to understand that the feeling of being in the Samadhi of Half-Dead resembles the state of "near death" where the surrounding engagement of "form, sound, smell, taste, touch, and mental phenomenon" and the functions of "eyes, ears, nose, tongue, body, and mind" all abruptly shrink. Any dharma realm of affinity can instantaneously be reached with a single thought of the mind.

I completely dwell between the realm of "thought" and "thoughtlessness," and experience the joy and sorrow of the respective dharma realm. Those who are not connected with me will run away from me, while those who have affinity with me can instantly be reached within a thought, even if they were thousands of miles away. The thought can transform naturally at will.

"Thought" is me and I am "thought." I experience things that seem real yet illusory, where reality can be described as neither existent nor empty.

Some people remark that this type of experience could be attributed to the "bardo body" phenomenon. Others say this is simple an out of body experience. Others regard this as a shift of consciousness. Nonetheless, I feel energized at times and occasionally a sense of heaviness weighs on me and I feel discouraged. This sense of discouragement arises from feelings of helplessness whenever I cannot deliver sentient beings, and visions manifested from their fear and the feelings of fear itself overcome me.

When I have exhausted my energy, when I am misunderstood, when I feel life is really an illusion, when I lose my sense of value and my sense of achievements, and when I am wronged by the world at large, I feel a similar sense of defeat in my spiritual travel.

Partaking in any spiritual travel is a unique spiritual experience which is very similar to meditation. I have documented my experiences in my book *Crossing the Ocean of Life and Death*, where I detailed how my physical body was disoriented due to my illness, somewhat dangling between life and death, throwing me into a situation where it was difficult to cope with everyday life.

I have cultivated throughout my entire life, but I am not a person who is rigid in my practice. I practice the extensive Vajrayana teachings and do not limit myself to one school of thought only. I am not lying. I gain expedient insights with my practice and my faith is not one built on blind faith.

I really have transformed the five desires of wealth, sex, fame, food and sleep into emptiness, hence, attaining the emptiness of body, emptiness of mind, emptiness of dharma, and emptiness of self-nature.

I have traveled to the ten dharma realms and countless buddha pure lands.

Zhuangzi said, "The man did not eat any of the five grains, but inhaled the wind and drank the dew; he mounted on the clouds, rode a flying dragon, wandering beyond the four seas."

Qu Yuen said, "Consuming the six energies and drinking the nightly dew, I rinse my mouth with yang itself and swallow morning light. Guarding the purity of the spirit light within, I absorb essence and energy, drive out all that's coarse. I sip the subtle fluid of the Flying Spring and hold the shining brightness of the Glittering Gem. My face, like jade, is flushed with radiant color; my pure essence is starting to grow strong."

My act of spiritual travel may be seen as spontaneously natural, pure and perhaps an achievement.

Well, if being spontaneous is living in inaction, my life since entering retreat at Leaf Lake, watching how the mountains change seasonally from green to yellow and yellow to green while I age through the years, is truly being in inaction. If my life is said to be pure, it is, as I socialize with no one. Right or wrong, success or failure has all turned into nothingness. It is indeed untainted. Speaking of achievements, little has been achieved, and I really feel a sense of helplessness.

For example, I once entered the "City of Unnatural Deaths" and saw an ex-disciple among the ghosts of unnatural death. He looked pitiful and I wanted to get close to save him, but as soon as I got close to him, he wouldn't pay attention to me. When I approached him from the east, he turned to the west. When I came from the south, he turned to the north. When I floated in the space above, he would lower his head and ignore me. I tried sticking my head out from the ground to reach him. Then he scolded me, "Sheng-yen Lu, what have you achieved? How dare you come to humiliate me?"

"Why don't you chant the Buddha's name and recite the mantra?"

"Look, Sheng-yen Lu, I don't need your sympathy. I don't want you to save me. I've seen enough of your tricks! What's the big deal?"

"Why don't you return to the Maha Twin Lotus Ponds?"

"No, the City of Unnatural Deaths is better than any other place.

Here, everybody is the same. It is all equal."

"Don't you want to believe that the Buddha can liberate sentient beings?"

"No."

I sighed, and said to myself, "Though the dharma gate is wide open, it can't save those without affinity!"

I wanted to stretch out my hand to empower him but he spit on me.

I left quietly and was extremely sad.

Here is a verse:

> **I know the Dharma realm of the ten directions like the palm of my hand**
> **This may seem an achievement, but it may not be so**
> **Reflecting on the disciple in the City of Unnatural Deaths**
> **Trying to save those without affinity is futile**

Here is another example:

I once traveled spiritually to a place called the "Black Death Kingdom." Why was it called "Black Death"? This was because the kingdom was pitch black and you couldn't even see your fingers in front of you. Hence, it is called "Black." Why was it called "Death"? The people here were all dead and lying straight like corpses. None of them were alive or had consciousness, hence it is called "Death." I lit up the place with my light emitting from my palm. I was taken aback at the sight of the corpses lying there.

I thought I could use my palm to emit light and empower the beings of "Black Death Kingdom." This light from my palm is very strong and when it enters into the hearts of sentient beings, it can produce power and energize them over a long time. This is the empowerment and blessings of the Vajrayana teachings.

I was hoping that the power of empowerment could merge with the people receiving it. I empowered a few of them but discovered that they did not make a single move. They showed no signs of revival.

I cried.

A buddha appeared and told me, "The beings of the Black Death Kingdom are truly dead. When people die, their next place of birth is usually determined by their karma, their habits, and their state of consciousness. The beings of Black Death Kingdom, however, have eliminated their karma and habits, and also completely extinguished their motivation in gaining rebirth. Therefore, they have cut their ties to birth and death much like a torn cloth. These souls would immediately arrive at the Black Death Kingdom and will never reborn again. This teaching was advocated by one of the six heretical masters who taught the non-existence of karma, habits, thoughts, and bodhicitta. Such is the nature of the Black Death Kingdom."

"Is there a cure?"

"No," said the buddha, who later left.

I felt dejected. The feeling of hopelessness weighed on me. Therefore, my advice to all practitioners is to generate the bodhicitta, for all salvation hinges on this wish to gain complete enlightenment.

I know the Dharma realm of the ten directions
like the palm of my hand
This may seem an achievement, but it may not
be so
Reflecting on the disciple in the City of
Unnatural Deaths
Trying to save those without affinity is futile

                              Sheng-yen Lu

10 The Five Deteriorating Signs of Heavenly Beings

I saw two celestial devakayas (angels) approaching me. Though they were very beautiful, they looked very scared. Even when they spoke, their voices trembled.

"Dear spiritual traveler, please stop. We would like to ask you a question."

I stopped, "How can I help you?"

"Are you Living Buddha Lian-sheng, Sheng-yen Lu?"

"Yes."

"Our lord would like to invite you."

"Who is your lord? How does he know me?"

"An ancient buddha told our lord that you would be passing by and that he should ask you to empower him with the lights from your palm, so that he can be saved. Therefore, our lord instructed us to wait for you here."

"Oh, I see."

I followed the devakayas to a place where grand pavilions stood, surrounded by white cranes, celestial beasts, exotic flowers and grasslands. It reflected a heavenly scene of exquisite beauty. The two devakayas brought me to see their lord.

When I saw him, I was astounded.

I noticed he had the five deteriorating signs of heavenly beings where the auric luminance had diminished, where his heavenly scent had lost its usual fragrance and the flowers on his body were fading away. His celestial garment was tainted, and he was unable to sit and sleep properly on his dharma throne and golden bed. He was definitely not himself.

Before me was a celestial lord whose hair has turned white and messy, whose sweat emitted a strong stench. He was weak and tears trickled down from his face. He seemed to have lost all his shine.

Good heavens! He had used up all of his good fortune and his karmic hindrances were appearing. These are the five deteriorating signs of celestial beings, much like a patient.

I asked, "Are you sick?"

"Yes," his voice appeared coarse and dull, tormented by his constant anguish.

I know when celestial beings have used up all of their good fortune, the five deteriorating signs will surely appear. I have seen this for myself. He was like a patient whose skin was coarse and whose hair was all white. He could neither sit nor stand still.

He looked pale and perplexed and did not know what to do.

The celestial wind was obviously comforting, yet he felt that it was piercing into his bone and causing him to wail in pain. The air was slightly warm, yet he felt boiling hot and was crying in pain!

I was astonished to see this.

The celestial lord said, "Living Buddha, I beg you to save me! I am completely debilitated and weak."

"How can I help you?"

"Through your empowerment and blessing. This was what the ancient buddha told me."

I said, "You should take refuge in the Root Guru, Buddha, Dharma and Sangha. You should repent for your indulgence in heavenly pleasure and for not generating bodhicitta. You should work diligently towards liberation for the attainment of the absolute dharma body."

"How should I do that?"

"Maintain a single-pointedness of mind. Practice the Six Paramitas and enter into the bodhisattva path."

The celestial lord begged piteously, "I will definitely follow your advice and do that."

All his attendants and devakayas kneeled and begged, "Please, Living Buddha Lian-sheng, Sheng-yen Lu, help us and our lord."

I stretched out my right hand. From the center of my palm, an intense light in the form of an OM Sanskrit seed syllable emitted and converged from the buddhas of the ten directions and the three times as well as all bodhisattvas and mahasattvas empowered the celestial lord; the light current was being directed to enter and flow through his entire celestial body.

The celestial lord cooperated with single mindedness of intent, allowing his being to merge with the light current, both interacting freely as they become one. He had extensive good fortune but all of it was depleted and he began to deteriorate, showing the five signs. If no one had saved him, he would have descended to the lower realm.

Luckily, through the guidance of the ancient buddha, I gave the empowerment to the celestial lord whose affinity with the Vasumitra, King Anala, and Jayoshmayatana was helpful to his awakening.

It was unfathomable. The faded blossom crown became invigorated; his aura brightened, the celestial garment was cleansed, fragrance filled the air, and he could sit and sleep at ease on his dharma seat and golden bed.

I said, "Buddhadharma initially unveils the true nature of the mind and elucidates the true cause for attaining buddhahood. Subsequently, one decides on the respective practice of the dharma of complete penetration which demonstrates the fine path to attaining buddhahood. And by moving through the sixty divine stages [of bodhisattvahood], completing the practice of bodhi, and eventually dwelling in the realization of non-attainment, one attains the ultimate fruition of buddhahood. When we align to buddhhood, we will be aware of the disturbances from the five maras, otherwise, the opposite holds true, where one falls into the seven states of sentient beings."

The celestial lord and his attendants nodded.

I told them, "The empowerment is only temporary. You must focus on practicing, accumulating immeasurable life, boundless light and incalculable merits. This is the right way. Exercise your own power at will that has already existed in you."

The celestial lord and his attendants all agreed to this.

The aura of the celestial lord restored in an instant. His heaven was illuminated by a dazzling display of lights, shining in the ultimate golden brilliance. The space was filled with an array of light much like the Indra's Net of Pearls. It could also be described as layers upon layers of fireworks display radiating in all directions. Like rainbows hanging in the sky, the seemingly endless rainbow hues decorated the entire sky. Exotic flowers and plants stemmed out everywhere, showing off their beauty.

Happiness filled the air in that heaven, and celestial music echoed in the entire realm just as celestial fragrance permeated the space. Divine nectar flowed ceaselessly like the stream, whose supply was abundant and endless. The good fortune of the celestial lord was in stored in abundance. He has been the lord for thousands of years until his karmic hindrances appeared, resulting in his appearance of deterioration. The buddhas of the ten directions and the three times, bodhisattvas and mahasattvas simply unlocked his store of good fortune, which after all, was his accumulation by his own effort. What I did was just unlocking it with my palm. As long as he sought to generate the bodhicitta and awake his consciousness, he could attain the fruition of bodhisattvahood and attain the Ten Paramitas.

I stealthily left the place, but was spotted by a devakaya. She said, "Your Holiness, Living Buddha, our gratefulness is unending. Why don't you stay behind and enjoy all the pleasures here."

Feeling somewhat sad, I replied, "I still have other unfinished business."

"Do you have any last advice for the lord and the rest of us?"

I sang a verse:

> **Do not say you have not seen the Buddha after your realization**
> **You must gain rebirth after you have attained realization**
> **A young child should learn from the teacher**
> **Just as a toddler must walk beside the mother**
> **You should realize that sufferings will make you appreciate practice**
> **Otherwise indulgence in pleasure will not lead to spiritual achievement**
> **Upon attaining thusness where there is non-birth**
> **One must return to the Saha world to deliver sentient beings**

After hearing the verse, the devakaya memorized it and related it to the celestial lord while I continued my spiritual travel.

Do not say you have not seen the Buddha after your realization
You must gain rebirth after you have attained realization
A young child should learn from the teacher
Just as a toddler must walk beside the mother
You should realize that sufferings will make you appreciate practice
Otherwise indulgence in pleasure will not lead to spiritual achievement
Upon attaining thusness where there is non-birth
One must return to the Saha world to deliver sentient beings

Sheng-yen Lu

11 Traveling over the Mountains and Rivers

I did not travel to any dharma realms this time in my spiritual travel. Instead, I traveled to the mountains and rivers of samsara.

I started out as a surveyor in my career as I studied geodetic survey in the university. Therefore, I have visited many mountains and rivers and have done a lot surveying work.

In fact, the mountains and rivers in this world are extremely beautiful. Otherwise, the beings of the Light Sound Heaven (Skt Abhasvara; Jpn Ko'on-ten) would not have descended to earth in the first place.

On earth, rivers meander naturally and the mountains are rippled. The South and North Poles, the sun, moon and stars, the high tide and low tide, the seasonal changes, the different cloud formations, and the airstreams are all simply amazing. I noticed that all physical phenomena on the surface each have its own energy field.

For example, the earth revolves around the sun on its orbit. The energy field of the moon affects the earth. The mountains and the rivers surround people, and they also have energy fields.

Apart from being a surveyor, I also studied feng shui. One should know that the earth is formed by the "earth wheel," "water wheel," "fire wheel," and "wind wheel." Humans are also composed of "earth, water, fire, and wind" elements. The earth and its people are closely related, and the same is also true for feng shui and people.

I know that the caves where Guru Naropa and Guru Padmasambhava practiced were connected to feng shui. There is no doubt that feng shui and practices are related.

People with good fortune live in places with good energy. This has everything to do with the bestowal of good merits.

I said:

> In hot tropical places, coconut trees exist.
>
> In desolated deserts, there is oil.

When I journeyed over the beautiful mountains and rivers, I had many feelings about the earth and felt it was really a good place to do cultivation. One can practice to achieve buddhahood, compassion, bodhi and blissfulness but people do not appreciate the earth. Instead, they engage in violence, greed, deception, and crimes which transgress the right teachings of the Buddha.

> **Do not commit bad deeds**
> **Perform all good deeds**
> **Purify your mind**
> **These are the Buddha's teachings**

There are wars, battles, disasters from water, fire, wind and earth, epidemics, the three major calamities, and the three minor calamities, among others, surrounding the beautiful mountains and rivers.

These mountains and rivers are all tainted with impurities. The spiritual energy from them has disappeared. Mountains and rivers are severely damaged. Nature has changed for the worse as damage is done to it. This is a setback for practitioners, who face many hardships. Should humans treat other humans like this?

In my early years of spreading the Dharma, I had suffered much harm and slander. I was young at that time and refuted every one of their criticism. Later, I practiced forbearance and through time, I became softened. No matter how people have tried to hurt me, I would not bear to retaliate. I was filled with compassion and concern for others, which naturally helped me enter into the Samadhi of Absent Dispute (Arana Samadhi). I did not dare to say bad, angry, and harsh words. I only wanted to propagate the True Buddha Tantra, to sow the dharma seeds in the world. I became a monk because I wanted to save people, to liberate them from suffering and allow them to gain happiness, for I could not bear to see them suffer. So, how could I have hatred for them?

While traveling spiritually, I saw calamity brewing in a certain place in the south-east. Out of compassion, and based on the Chinese's Eight Diagrams of corresponding natural phenomena of sky (qian), earth (kun), thunder (zhen), wind (xun), lake (dui), water (kan), fire(li), mountain (gen), I inhaled a mouthful of qi from the Xun direction (south-west) in an attempt to build up a gust of divine wind and blow away the evil energy. When I was inhaling, however, three sages came out from the south-east and said,

"You can't do it. You can't do it, Lian-sheng."

I bowed in respect to the three sages and asked, "Why?"

"It is an inexorable fate!"

"I am a practitioner and I can't bear to see sentient beings suffer. I want to get rid of their inexorable fate. Isn't this what compassion is all about?"

I continued, "Does it make any sense that you're not going to help people who are in trouble? Isn't this a contradiction to cultivation?"

The sages said, "This is group karma!"

The three sages pointed towards the many banners strewn across the mountains and rivers, which meant this calamity was commanded by divine will. I was astonished.

Too many people in this world go against their conscience, for they kill, they steal, and they swindle for their own gains. There are just too many evil people and collectively they create group karma. Calamities and human disasters will soon befall on them. These people are still day-dreaming!

The majority of people never know cultivation. They work for the sake of food, clothing, shelter, travel, education, and entertainment. They struggle against each other, creating chaos in the family, society, and country. Their greed is immeasurable, turning their back on enlightenment for material pursuit. This will surely attract calamities and human disasters!

I sighed. I cried over and over again with tears streaming down my face.

I put my palms together and paid respect to the three sages. They left and disappeared.

I remembered that the Golden Mother of the Jade Pond once took me to a lake during the early years of my cultivation. The lake's reflection revealed a vision of my future and that of the earth itself. I was shocked to learn that my future was full of calamities, so was the world we live in. Calamities and human disasters were only part of my vision but it was enough to cause great agony to me. How unfortunate is the human world to suffer such disasters? How many people have died in the hands of death?

What catastrophes we must go through!

Life and death are predestined.

Wealth and social status hinge on heaven's will.

It is about time human beings repent. We should be shameful [for lingering in life and death]; fearful [of the wheel of reincarnation]; hold thoughts of revulsion from attachment; aspire for enlightenment; show equanimity to our enemies; be grateful to the Buddha; and contemplate on the empty nature of transgression.

Human beings should not indulge in ceaseless accumulation of material wealth. When you gain the whole world, you will lose your place in the heavens. What you should really accumulate is divine wealth which includes the wealth of faith, the wealth of diligence, the wealth of discipline, the wealth of repentance, the wealth of learning and charity, the wealth of patience, and the wealth of concentration and wisdom.

One must believe in the True Buddha Tantra. If you have doubts you cannot practice it. The True Buddha Tantra can really help you to reach the other shore. I have attained through it. I can truly guarantee and validate the completion of the teaching and practice. If you have doubts, it will surely hinder your practice and you will not be successful.

If you don't believe me, you can simply practice the Pure Land teaching, or at least believe what the Buddha had said, that by chanting the Buddha's name single-mindedly, committing your body and mind to gaining rebirth in the Western Paradise of Ultimate Bliss. This is when true emptiness is finally realized through the function of the illusory form, where one attains the state of non-birth!

One must believe in the True Buddha Tantra. If you have doubts you cannot practice it. The True Buddha Tantra can really help you to reach the other shore. I have attained through it. I can truly guarantee and validate the completion of the teaching and practice.

Sheng-yen Lu

12 The Merit of Spiritual Traveling

I once met someone in my spiritual travel who accompanied me. He had three lights above his head that were divine lights. These lights lit up the sky as we traveled, whose strength could even penetrate through the dense darkness of the netherworld. It was truly amazing.

I asked him, "How do you gain the three divine lights above your head?"

He answered, "By focusing on accumulating and retaining merits."

"How do you accomplish that?"

The sage answered, "I feed the hungry, heal the sick, and enhance people's fortune and wisdom. That is why I have these three divine lights."

I admired him. Just accomplishing these three feats are more than enough to accumulate good merits.

The sage said, "Living Buddha Lian-sheng, Sheng-yen Lu, your merit and virtue accumulated through spiritual travel are impressive too. Why do you admire me?"

"I don't really have any merit. I am very ashamed of myself. Just like the Buddha said, we came to the world to repay karma, to work off karma. I consider myself a person who is indebted with heavy negative karma and have had a great number of mishaps, so much so that I am almost drowned by them. I feel I am incapable of saving sentient beings, so what merits do I have? I really feel ashamed."

I thought about many charitable organizations in the world whose efforts have received praise from around the world. The bigger the blessings are, the greater their merits. The smaller the blessings are, the smaller their merits. Competing among themselves, wouldn't merit and virtue be reduced to a measure of blessings? That would be some cause and effect.

People such as I, who stumble through life riding through the ups and downs, don't even have time to take care of myself, let alone remedy my previous karma, present karma, and future karma. So, how can I dwell on merits? I can only ask my conscience, "How much karma have I really created?" So how can I even think about any merit and virtue at all?

I also thought about the *Diamond Sutra* which states that those who speak of having merit have no merit for true merit exists as non-attachment to so called merit.

I smiled wryly. Suddenly three divine lights appeared on my head.

The sage explained, "One light represents truthfulness, the other one represents honesty, and the last one represents diligence. Merit cannot be sought, but it exists within oneself."

I was surprised, "Why do I also have three divine lights?"

The sage said, "Your actions reflect your mind. Your mind is truthful. You don't have an evil mind. You are always genuinely compassionate and have concern for others. Therefore, the first light you have represents truthfulness."

The sage continued, "When you meet bad people who did bad deeds and received their punishments, you save them equally. You never discriminate between who to save and who not to save. You vow not to abandon a single sentient being including those in the animal realm, whom you helped to deliver to the Amitabha's Pure Land by chanting the Deliverance Mantra or chant the name Namo Amitabha Buddha to help them gain rebirth in the Pure Land. You treat all sentient beings equally. This represents your second divine light. It is the light of honesty."

The sage ended by saying, "The third divine light is the light of diligence. You never stop practicing and never stop writing to deliver sentient beings. It is very rare now to find a person with such perseverance in this world. It is rare to find a true practitioner who remains sincere and diligent in his cultivation amidst the mountains of mara's tests that come one's way. Furthermore, you have abandoned all material indulgences in wealth, sex, fame, food, and sleep. The more obstructions there are, the more diligent you become. This is the way to learn and practice Buddhism. This is the third divine light."

I told the sage, "I have heard that merit is gained by carrying out good deeds, saving the world through compassion, giving wealth, building temples and making offerings. The field of merit and virtue is one of the three fields of cultivating merits for the act of paying homage and making offerings to the Triple Gem, the Buddha, Dharma and Sangha, which will attract immeasurable blessings. Then there are the fragrance of merit and virtue, such as the fragrance of discipline, fragrance of concentration, fragrance of wisdom, fragrance of liberation, and fragrance of awareness of liberation. These five kinds of fragrance of merits will lead to the manifestation of the dharmakaya truth body."

The sage responded, "That is correct. You also accumulated merit from your spiritual traveling!"

I asked, "What merit does spiritual traveling have?"

The sage replied, "Spiritual traveler Living Buddha Lian-sheng, Sheng-yen Lu, you have exercised patience in good and bad situations. You have conquered the defiled nature of your mind. You reach out to save people when the circumstances and affinity arise. Your heart is soft, kind, and accommodating. You are able to fit in among the mundane and make them feel you are part of them. Whether you are dealing with sentient beings or non-sentient lives, or those with or without affinity, you are compassionate to all of them knowing all are in oneness. The expression of movement and stillness are in harmony with true thusness. This is the merit of spiritual traveling."

I responded, "I feel ashamed. I have no merit and I am incapable."

Here we were, two people with six divine lights.

As we traveled across space, we did appear impressive.

We flew over Purvavideha (half moon shape, eastern continent of Mount Meru), Jambudvipa (human face shape, southern continent of Mount Meru), Godaniya (round shape, western continent of Mount Meru) and Uttarakuru (square shape, northern continent of Mount Meru).

We passed Mount Meru, a marvellous high mountain. The mountain is composed of gold, silver, lazurite, and crystal. That is why it is marvellous. All other mountains are lower than Mount Meru. That is why it is high. Mount Meru is 84,000 yojanas [one yojana equals eight miles] high and wide. It is the king of all mountains.

Mount Meru is the polar centre of a small cosmic complex [of seas and mountains]. Its top and base is big, while narrowing at the centre [shaped like an hourglass]. The four deva kings reside at the mid-lower slopes on each side of the mountain. Trayastrimsa Heaven is located at the apex of the mountain. At the base, there are seven circles of golden mountain ranges and seven circles of fragrant seas surrounding the mountains. Beyond the gold mountain ranges, there is the salt water sea. Beyond the salt water sea, there is the iron encircling mountain. The four great continents are each situated at the four directions of the salt water sea.

When we arrived at Trayastrimsa Heaven, we did not see the lord of this heaven. Instead, we saw somebody else. This person had thousands of lights on top of his head. The two of us only had six lights combined, but yet he had countless lights.

I was shocked, "It must be the Indra's Net of Luminous Pearls."
The sage clarified, "No, it is my master."
"Who is your master?"
"The Merit Retaining Jewel King Buddha."
I was really surprised. Why did this Buddha show up at Trayastrimsa Heaven?

The sage answered, "Don't be surprised. I am the emanation of the Merit Retaining Jewel King Buddha," and then he flew into the heart of the Buddha.

The Merit Retaining Jewel King Buddha wanted me to remember this verse:

> **The superior man exercises his mind**
> **In the most open and pure manner**
> **Extinguishing all mental cognition of external things**
> **We are able to let go and be**
> **As we connect with all life**
> **Where the affinity lies**
> **We shall always see the Tathagata**

My encounter with the Merit Retaining Jewel King Buddha at Trayastrimsa Heaven left me even more cautious and conscientious, knowing that at anytime I could meet a spiritual traveler or a spiritual friend who might be a great bodhisattva, an enlightened buddha. This could not be overlooked.

Verses in *The Jewel-Nature Treatise* (*Ratnagotravibhāga-mahāyānôttaratantra-śāstra*) state:

> **Like buddhas abiding in withering lotus flowers**
> **Like gold buried among impurities**
> **Like treasures under the ground**
> **Like sprouts grown from fruits**

> Like a golden statue wrapped in a tattered garment
> Like the wheel-turning sage king in the womb of a poor ugly woman
> And like a precious statue in the earthen mould
> Among sentient beings obscured by greed, anger and ignorance
> As well as occasional stains of defilements
> In all states of pollution
> One finds the Essence of the Tathagata
> Even at the Avici Hell
> The body of the Tathagata is seen
> The Dharma of Pure Thusness
> Is thus called the nature of Tathagata

Once I saw an old lady who was very ugly, with protruding eyes, bizarre ears, a twisted mouth, and a hunched back. When she was traveling, she was really hopping up and down about a foot high from the grassland. When I observed her, she had the appearance of a junior ranking earth deity. Being an earth deity was fine as she could have been a yaksa, an old raksasa, or even an evil spirit. I noticed her and she noticed me.

Then she rolled her eerie eyes and laughed. Her whole body was extremely filthy. She even recognized me and spoke, "Living Buddha Lian-sheng, Sheng-yen Lu, how are you? I'll talk to you when I have time."

I ignored her and in a way, looked down upon her. I didn't feel like talking to her and she didn't mind. She went around from one house to the next, distributing medicine to people who were sleeping. I didn't think it was anything special to make rounds around houses, giving away medicine to the villagers in the middle of the night. Would her act be considered as good deed? Or perhaps just an act of mischief?

When the old lady finished, she soared into the sky and instantly transformed into Avalokitesvara (Guanyin Bodhisattva), the Mahasattva who constantly observes the world and liberates sentient beings from suffering and bestow them with happiness. So long as people call upon her name, she answers their prayers and helps them. Her origin is the Tathagata of Clear Understanding of the Dharma. She rides the deva naga and her body radiates light. She has the majestic look of a Buddha.

I felt deeply ashamed.

I highly praised Avalokitesvara for her majestic appearance and great compassion to liberate sentient beings!

The Bodhisattva simply said, "Here in this village, this is how I choose to appear."

My heart cried out, "Shame on me! Shame on me!"

When the old lady finished, she soared into the sky and instantly transformed into Avalokitesvara (Guanyin Bodhisattva), the Mahasattva who constantly observes the world and liberates sentient beings from suffering and bestow them with happiness. So long as people call upon her name, she answers their prayers and helps them. Her origin is the Tathagata of Clear Understanding of the Dharma. She rides the deva naga and her body radiates light. She has the majestic look of a Buddha.

Sheng-yen Lu

13 Grief

I flew over the Hell of Great Wailing.

The reason it was called the Hell of Great Wailing was due to the high torment experienced by the suffering beings there, who cried loudly and miserably.

As I heard them wailing pitifully, I grieved. The Hell of Great wailing was a real nightmare.

What a pity these beings were!

The outcome of death is dust to dust, earth to earth, but it also includes consciousness to consciousness and spirit to spirit.

How do we assess and weigh the beginningless and endless cycle of life and death, the causes and effects, and the karmic retributions? Sages with the power to understand previous lives would also find it difficult to completely comprehend these karmas.

In the Hell of Great Wailing, I saw a young student of mine. He was only twenty-five years old and he was a recent university graduate. He was young and handsome, but he passed away.

When he died, he neither went to the Western Paradise of Ultimate Bliss nor the heavens. Instead, he fell into the lower three paths of the hell realm. I was very sad.

I asked, "How did you die?"

"Leukemia."

I recognized him and asked, "How did you end up in the Hell of Great Wailing. You are a True Buddha practitioner!"

"I only took refuge recently."

"Have you chanted the Four Refuge Mantra?"

"No."

"What about other practices?"

"No."

I knew his soul consciousness did not receive the empowerment. Taking refuge was simply done in name only. The actual refuge of the spiritual consciousness depends on the practice right from the beginning, in order to receive the empowerment from the buddhas and deities. This empowerment needs to come from one's own practice, by accumulating good fortune, and by cleansing karmic hindrances. Up to that point, however, he did not cultivate and as a result he descended into the Hell of Great Wailing of the hell realm. This was very pitiful.

Such is:

> **The Tao being what it is**
> **Encompasses life and death between heaven and earth**
> **While it constantly nurtures all living things**
> **Birth is inescapable**
> **So is death**
> **And no sage can possible name this Tao**

I asked him, "Why did you receive such retribution?"

He answered, "I killed a sage in my past life."

I was extremely grieved. This was tragic because it was one of the Seven Heinous Deeds which are: killing one's father, mother, or an arhat, spilling a buddha's blood, disrupting the harmony of the community of monks, killing a monk or an acharya.

He said, "This sage was an acharya. I misunderstood him and killed him. I was supposed to fall into the Avici Hell but due to the fact that I took refuge, I ended up in the Hell of Great Wailing. Even if I yell and scream here, it will not do anything to help my suffering."

He added, "This is the fourth hell of the Eight Hot Hells. Here, beings scream with excruciating pain because they cannot tolerate the pain they experience."

I saw the following punishments:
> Forced to swallow heated metal balls,
> Burned as they were dying of thirst,
> Fried in copper woks,
> Flushed with fire and smoke through their noses.

I was extremely sorrowful. This was very painful to watch!

The student kneeled and bowed to me. He begged, "Since Grand Master Living Buddha Lian-sheng is here, you must save me from this hell."

I asked him, "Do you know this?"

> **If one wishes to know**
> **The buddhas of the three times**
> **They should observe the nature of the dharma realm**
> **That everything is the creation of the mind**

He responded, "I don't understand this verse."

I repeated again, "Do you know that if you want to gain rebirth in the Amitabha Buddha's Pure Land and transcend all suffering, you have to have faith, make vows, and practice the dharma by chanting Namo Amitabha Buddha?"

"How do I have faith, make vows, and practice the dharma?" (He didn't even know that believing in Amitabha Buddha and making vows would allow him to be reborn in the Western Paradise.)

I said, "The Hell of Great Wailing belongs to the Fire Hell. You should learn that pure fire cleanses the mind, quiet fire tones one's nature, stable fire empties all things, and true inner fire is samadhi."

He answered, "I don't know how to do that."

I taught him again, "The truth about soul is to realize its unique spiritual nature, and by using the elements of earth, water, fire, and wind, you as soul gets rid of all mental afflictions and suffering. As long as your heart realizes emptiness, attains liberation, and enters infinite bliss, you will be able to sever yourself from the constraints of the fire hell and be free from it."

"I am unable to understand this."

I taught him again, "Extinguish your desire, and then you will be able to control the fire. Keep your body, speech, and mind purified, and the fire shall become pure and cool. Pray for the empowerment of Amitabha Buddha, focus your mind upon the Western Paradise and receive the joy of being reborn in the Pure Land. You will attain the ultimate liberation. Dedicate your strength to liberate sentient beings so that they can enter the bodhi path. Free yourself from the grip of worldly affairs and turn yourself into the master of the Threefold Body (trikaya or three bodies of a Buddha)."

(I had already explained this very clearly.)

What a pity. He still had the fire of fury. He resented losing his life at such a young age. This was the fruit of anger, being angry at the acharya, being angry at losing his lover, and being angry about many other things.

He couldn't meditate on emptiness. He couldn't purify his body, speech, and mind.

I went to see Lord Yama and begged him to save my student.

Lord Yama responded, "Do you know the karmic causes of this student?"

"No, I never looked into it." I admitted.

Lord Yama explained, "He committed the worst of the seven misdeeds, which was killing a sagacious archarya in his previous life, and this archarya was none other than you, Living Buddha Lian-sheng."

I almost fainted when I heard that.

Lord Yama said, "You have made your vow not to abandon a single sentient being. You do not differentiate between anyone and attempt to save them all equally. This is why you ran into countless mishaps in all your lifetimes. Since this is how his karmic conditions were created, there is nothing you can do about it."

I felt dejected but I will wait until he has finished his sentence. I still want to save him.

I recited a verse:

> **As we enter samadhi we deliver those who are lost**
> **We practice the path without hesitation all day and night**
> **Delivering all diligently knowing the reality of non-birth**
> **Hand in hand we travel along the pond of Seven Treasures**

**If one wishes to know
The buddhas of the three times
They should observe the nature of the dharma realm
That everything is the creation of the mind**

Sheng-yen Lu

14 Spiritual Travels as Influenced by Possession

In the *Samyuktavadana Sutra* (*Sutra on the Miscellaneous Collection of Metaphors*) I read an account whose story is similar to spiritual travel. However, it is not a genuine case of spiritual travel but one influenced through spirit possession. I particularly wanted to write about this and cite it as a cautionary tale.

There was once a bhiksu (monk) who had broken a major precept and was expelled from the monastery. In addition, all of the followers abandoned him, causing him to feel extremely remorseful and feel like he had no way out.

While he was crying and walking around sadly, a ghost saw him. The ghost had also broken a precept and was thrown out by the Vaisravana, the All-Hearing Deva-King, one of the Four Heavenly Kings. The ghost was traveling speedily when he saw the crying monk.

The ghost asked, "Why are you crying?"

The bhiksu replied, "I committed a great sin in the monastery and was expelled. Also, the temple's followers rejected me and I no longer received offerings. I lost everything I had. Now I am penniless and I have a bad reputation that spreads widely. I don't have anywhere to stay."

The ghost declared, "I am a mighty ghost of great power. I can perform spiritual travel and I can help you to clear up your bad name, restore your reputation, and help you receive huge offerings."

The bhiksu asked, "How do I do that?"

The ghost explained, "You can stand on my left shoulder and I will fly with you. It will look like you are walking in the air. People will only be able to see you flying and they won't see me. That will show them your ability. This way, you will regain your reputation and also receive offerings from the public. But, you must share the offerings with me."

The bhiksu replied, "Alright!"

Subsequently, the mighty ghost carried the bhiksu and circled over the monastery. All the monks watched and they were dumbfounded, awestruck at the sight.

The pair then went into the town, flying around and walking in the air as though there was a flat surface below. Word of it spread from one person to another. People came out of their houses and rushed to watch with great astonishment as the bhiksu circled in the air. They conceded that he did not breach any precept and instead, was an accomplished sage who was innocent.

Furthermore, the followers in the town agreed that the monastery was at fault and that the bhiksu had been wrongly accused. They welcomed the bhiksu to return to the monastery and allowed him to live there again. He was appointed to a respectful position and he received offerings many times more than what he used to receive.

The bhiksu was very happy and he did not forget his promise. He shared the offerings with the mighty ghost and the mighty ghost was also delighted. They both continued to work together, until one day when something went wrong.

There are Six Exclusionary Times in the heaven. The eighth and twenty-third days are supervision days. The fourteenth and thirtieth days are the prince days, and the first and fifteenth days are the days when the Four Heavenly Kings travel [these are the times when ghosts are not permitted to travel].

The mighty ghost forgot about the fifteenth day. On that day, he picked up the bhiksu and flew in the air freely. At that time, Vaisravana, the Heavenly King (Guardian of the North) was on duty making his circuit. When the mighty ghost saw his master, he was stunned and scared to death. He immediately let go of the bhiksu and scurried away, never daring to look back. The bhiksu was happy and free in the air but he was unexpectedly dropped by the mighty ghost. The bhiksu didn't have time to react and dropped straight to the ground; his head and body smashed against a big rock, and he died instantly. Immediately, his spirit was drawn into the three lower realms and reincarnated.

(The above story was an example of spiritual travel under influence of an external force.)

According to my knowledge, our human bodies can be possessed by spirits, sometimes by more than one. The affects of evil spirit possession will appear on that person's face as a tint of dark energy, grey smoke, and dull aura. If the person is possessed by evil spirits from the netherworld or hell realm, then he can be taken to the dark realm.

When a person is possessed by an animal spirit, his body will have emitted a fishy stench. If a person is possessed by an elemental entity, then he will display some psychic phenomena.

Once a person is possessed, his soul may be taken on a journey, most of which will happen during his sleep. Traveling spiritually at night and waking up in the day will make him very tired. He can never gain control of himself, and will always be taken around and flying aimlessly in his chaotic dreams.

Spiritual traveling by possession is not only carried out by ghosts, animal spirits and elemental entities but also by deceased relatives, haunting spirits, demonic spirits, and even foetus spirits. Many people who travel in their dream are subjected to such influence.

This form of spiritual traveling by possession is generally unable to reach the angelic realms, the heavenly realms or the holy realms. The best that they can do is to take a trip to the angelic realm. Usually they travel to supra-physical realm above or below the physical plane, or descend to the netherworld. They cannot control their own travel. They are just being led around. (If any made it to the angelic or heavenly realm, it would be seen as a rare occurrence.)

If a person is possessed during the day and night, then this is a case of mental disorder.

I have seen many people possessed by animal spirits, mountain demons and aquatic creatures, and spirits of wrongful death, being led to travel in their sleep. This kind of journey by possession is not good. Sometimes the karmic creditors come to possess the body periodically. This results in an endless entanglement of dreams filled with greed. Malevolent spirits are indeed everywhere. This world, shrouded by karmic hindrances, is heavily polluted by desires. Practitioners must perform the Eightfold Paths, but they also face a considerable amount of obstacles.

Honestly speaking, greed is the root cause for the six realms of reincarnation. Whether one is a human or a ghost, when there are too much greed and attachment, such indulgence and fixation to desire and anger, would result in the intention to continue previous relationships, or wanting to take revenge, thus forming the cause and effect of reincarnations.

Consequently, there are joy and sorrow, reunion and parting, birth and death, and the convergence of all sufferings.

We all know that excessive desire is the root cause of suffering. Reducing desire and practicing transcendence will lead to complete freedom. Sentient beings are subjected to emotional entanglement. That's why they suffer. Humans and ghosts are the same. Though they may be aware of the pitfalls of emotion, they have a difficult time seeing through the illusions of the world. Therefore, everyone is bound by emotional attachments. (Compassionate bodhisattvas must transform their mind upon approaching every situation in order to free themselves from being tied up.)

Practitioners who wish to avoid possession by spirits in their spiritual travel must observe the following:

    Reduce desires and simple be.
    Let go of desire and passion.
    Rest in no matter and no mind.
    Let go of wealth and fame.
    Go with the flow and be at peace.
    Be satisfied and go with the flow.
    Remain unmoved as it is.
    Practice the Eightfold Paths.
    Be as great as the dharma realm.
    Be as wide as the sea and sky.

I once came upon a student who was spiritual traveling. In his travel he was possessed by a powerful demon from the mara realm. The powerful mara was dressed in a black robe, and he had led my disciple into the wrong paths, entangling him with little chance of escape. The disciple was possessed during the day as well as through the night, and his family thought he had lost his mind. As a result, he was sent to a mental hospital where he continued to hallucinate and hear voices. His hallucination was really bad. He talked nonsense, channelled automatic writing, acted as a medium, jumped and hopped around erratically, shouting, crying and screaming. One moment his soul went up the heaven and the next moment, he descended to hell. Next moment he wanted to help people resolve their problems.

His normal life was thrown into chaos. He thought that he could not be drowned, burned, or penetrated by knives and bullets. He felt he was greater than the Buddha.

While traveling spiritually, I saw that he was possessed.

I shouted loudly, "Don't make a fool of my student!"

The mara said, "You know me?"

"How could I not recognize you? You are the witty demon of meditation. You are the mara of samadhi, indulging in your own meditation."

As soon as he heard me, he was aware that I knew him very well and he desperately ran away. I saved the student's soul, and merged his soul consciousness and body back into one again. I then sealed his body's openings to prevent his soul from getting out again (known as Boundary Protection). After this he was cleansed, he returned to his normal life, and never drifted off again. He abandoned all evil deeds and resumed his life as a normal practitioner.

After he awoke, he told people, "I was bewitched by mara, but Grand Master came and saved me."

"How did he save you?"

"Grand Master chased the mara away and retrieved my consciousness."

The man's family thanked Grand Master.

Some people who are possessed think that they have supernatural power but in fact, this kind of phenomenon is just a form of assisted power. If it is not severe, it can be looked at as a form of mysticism. In this case, the space dimension undergoes transformation and this can be a subject of study, but one must approach it with the correct view to do so!

15 Devil Realm

I once ventured into the mara or devil realm in my spiritual travel. The ten maras are:

Mara of the Aggregates - This mara works through the transformation of the five aggregates of form, feeling, perception, action and consciousness and is the root cause of all transgressions.

Mara of Defilements - Creates disturbance in one's mind, and bending truth.

Mara of Karma - Create karma in killing, stealing, lust, and lying, ending up as a mara.

Mara of the Mind - Become a mara due to doubt, vanity and arrogance.

Mara of Death - Taking the physical as well as spiritual lives of men.

Mara of the Celestial Realm - The celestial lord of the sixth heaven, which creates hindrance to men generating good thoughts.

Mara of Benevolence - Attached to the idea of doing good, but lack the motivation to advance spiritually.

Mara of Samadhi - Attachment to meditation, lacking the intention to seek enlightenment.

Mara of Knowledge - A hoarder of the knowledge of Dharma, but unwilling to deliver sentient beings.

Mara of Bodhi Dharma Wisdom - Attachment to the teachings of bodhi, wise in its ways, but creates hindrances to the path of liberation.

(The line between buddha and mara is sometimes separated only by a single thought or thread.)

There, in the mara realm, I saw four maras sitting and reading poetry:

> **Samsara is full of turmoil**
> **Nothing like our realm which is peaceful and nurturing**
> **Where suffering and joy could never touch**
> **Thus it is called unhindered and most capable**
>
> **The absence of complete death and birth is called non-birth**
> **Taking rebirth is incompatible to non-birth**
> **The buddha and mara are really one**
> **By differentiating between the two, when will Tao be attained**
>
> **The wisdom of Manjushri is false and empty**
> **Nagarjuna's arguments are simply clumsy**
> **Let me say this to the true practitioner**
> **Who in the world is not a fool**
>
> **When speaking of truth, how much is really truth**
> **When any reasoning misses the mark, the reason cannot be established**
> **The untainted and tainted are all dust**
> **Entering such samadhi is truly confusing**

The four verses appeared to make sense but had deviated somehow from the truth. The four maras then saw me approaching them.

One mara said, "This Living Buddha Lian-sheng, Sheng-yen Lu recognized me the other day, so I had to leave."

The other three maras were indignant.

"Shall we tie him up?"

"That would be easy," the samadhi mara said.

"How?"

"Living Buddha Lian-sheng, Sheng-yen Lu is a very affectionate person. We can use the 'passion cord' to tie him up. That's how easy it is."

So a cord was ejected from the centre of the palm of each mara which tied around me, binding me tightly. I totally lost my senses.

These cords worked very well on my weaknesses.

The first was the emotional cord of family bond.

The second was the emotional cord of affectionate love.

The third was the emotional cord of guru and student relationship.

The fourth was the emotional cord towards sentient beings.

The samadhi mara laughed, "Living Buddha Lian-sheng, Sheng-yen Lu could not shake off these affections. These cords are the easiest ways to tie him down. This guy is being hard-pressed by affection, and is always sad, groaning and mourning, and crying in pain. We maras want to see how he can possibly break free from this net of emotion."

The other three maras laughed, "This sentimental fool is being bound by other stone cold earthlings. Haha!"

The samadhi mara sneered at me, "Some Casanova you are."

The other three maras jeered, "Here's one sicko of love."

I was trapped in the evil net. This could be my karmic retribution because I cannot possibly fulfill my vows to deliver all sentient beings. My connection with sentient beings is too deep. I incarnate again and again, lifetimes upon lifetimes, to save sentient beings. How can my feelings for sentient beings cease when sentient beings remain un-awakened?

The bond between guru and student is deep. I have five million students. Their faults are my responsibility. My merits and good fortunes are insufficient to repay their karmic debts. When students behave out of line, how can I turn a blind eye to them? I am not someone who can possibly forget the bond between guru and student.

Love for family and loved ones is the most basic feeling. My parents in this life, Master Lianxiang who assists me in delivering sentient beings, and my son and daughter are people that I have connected with throughout many lifetimes. How can I abandon them?

Just these three things are enough to tie me down.

Finally when talking about emotion, I am a compassionate bodhisattva. Emotion cannot be seen, heard or touched but it can express itself as bio current, as thought, and as feeling. When I was in my youth, I could never release myself from the emotional bonds. I know it is difficult to get out of the emotional entanglement, but as a practitioner you have to struggle out of it, otherwise you will fall. It is hard to understand this emotional thing as it is difficult to handle as the tinkling sensation from some emotion is really unimaginable.

The four strings of cord were really tight around me. I was desperate and I could not break through this evil net. The cords wrapped themselves all around me.

The net tightened further and further, and I was in great pain. I thought that these four kinds of affections were the products of my affinities. A practitioner must become the master of all causes and effects, and not be controlled by these affinities. To relieve the pain and suffering of these affections, the mind must be very pure and clear. The body, speech, and mind must be extremely purified and the practitioner must be able to transform them to attain permanent bliss.

The transformation can be the transcendence from trivial love to great love, to express great compassion for all regardless of the affinity, as we are all one. Affection between family members and loved ones, between guru and students, should all be transformed into the universal love for all sentient beings. Work hard to deliver all sentient beings, but do not indulge in keeping count. This is the essence of wisdom.

One must be able to embrace and let go. Then you truly are the master (a practitioner who is the master of himself).

When I realized this point, a great spiritual energy was released from inside of me, sending forth enormous bright light like the incomparable light of great wisdom. **OM AH HUM**. The four cords snapped all at once. All of my innate power from my cultivation was released; its great luminance light up all directions. The four maras froze.

I stood up immediately and chanted, "Namo the thirty-six trillion, one hundred and nineteen thousand, and five-hundred Amitabha Buddhas."

I understood illusion. I learned to accept my responsibilities, and let go of all grasping. I am not attached to anything.

The samadhi mara said, "It looks like I will have to run away again."

The other three maras said, "This person radiates green light, red light, purple light, yellow light, golden light, orange light, and white light. He has transformed into the rainbow body. Let's split!"

This can be expressed as:

> **Touching my buddha with my heart**
> **My buddha responds immediately**
> **The response is either earlier nor later**
> **As my mind and buddha are really one**

I know the *Sutra on the Bodhisattva's Avoidance of Lust* writes:

> **Sexual lust is like a chain that holds society bondage. Ordinary people lust after it so much that they cannot escape from it.**
>
> **Sexual lust is a serious transgression of society. Ordinary people are so enclosed by it that they cannot let go of it even upon death.**

Sexual lust is a misfortune that once encountered will attract all tragedies to oneself.

If the practitioner can part with this lust, knowing it is a release from hell, yet continue to think of getting back into the action, much like a mad person whose madness is stopped, yet he wants to continue with his madness, or a patient whose illness has deteriorated, yet he cannot bear to be healed. The wise takes pity on him, yet knowing the practitioner's madness, is doomed to death in no time.

Ordinary people are fixated on lust, and are willing to become slaves. They toil and sweat their whole lives, suffering willingly even as lust drills and cut through their bodies like iron drills and a thousand knives. Yet they don't see lust as a cause for concern, dwelling in its pleasure like a mad man indulging in his joy of madness.

If the practitioner can let go of his attachment to sexual lust, then he would be free from bondage, leaving his madness and illness for good, he would be free from his misfortunes. He shall enjoy peace and auspiciousness like the prisoner being released from the prison, never to have misfortunes.

A woman's appearance is such that her words may be as sweet as honey, but her heart can be poisonous. Like a clear and calm pond lives the dragons; like a gold mountain and treasure cave is home to the lions, beware of this danger and stay away from it.

Disharmony in the family is caused by women. Disgrace and destruction to one's ancestors and clans are often attributed to women. They are like stealthy thieves who destroy the wisdom of people. They are like hunters who set traps that few can escape from. They are like nets set in high areas that trap birds, preventing them from flying away. They are also like interwoven fish nets that catch fishes, and once they are caught, the fishes shall end up having their bellies gouged and their flesh chopped. They are like dark pits that people can't see and fall into. And men are like moths rushing to the fire. Hence, the wise knows the harm lust brings and stays far away. Then they will not be harmed and affected by these filthy things.

The Buddha expounded this verse in the *Maharatnakuta Sutra*, the *Great Jewel-Heap Sutra*:

> Women are capable of inflicting pain on people, like razor-sharp blades cutting up a mountain or pains like those caused from a poison arrow
> Through the disguise of offering incense and flower as adornment, fools are led to accept these offerings
> These fools are like tired sea birds lost at sea, hoping to land on the distant shore. When they die, they will surely descend into Avici Hell
> Upon seeing all kinds of suffering gather upon one, virtuous friends drift away and entry into the heavens is lost forever
> One would rather descend into hell, run across blade mountains, and sleep inside furnaces, than get close to women

When I read the verse, I was deeply awakened. Women are absolutely scary. Lust is scary. My cord of sentiment naturally broke and disappeared.

The Buddha's verse reminded me of an early ancestor from the Lu family name lineage named "Jiang Ziya," who sang this verse:

> **The fangs of a bamboo snake**
> **The sting of a yellow wasp**
> **Is nothing when compared**
> **To the viciousness of a woman's heart**

I really didn't have much to say after reading the verses of Buddha and Jiang Ziya. Perhaps these ancient comments are unjust to women but I find myself almost at a loss of words when it comes to defending for women.

When I was caught by the mara's net, I realized that family love, affectionate love, love between guru and disciple, as well as love for sentient beings, are all momentary illusions. This is actually a world of illusion. Everyone is in an illusive grasp for passion and romance, like a shadow running after another shadow. After death, all forms of emotional love will simply return to the ocean of karma.

Only the buddhas and bodhisattvas are able to use affection to develop endless compassion and wisdom, carrying out salvation in all given opportunities, leading to the complete tranquility of form and mind.

I would advise the unwavering practitioners to avoid the following:

The causes of lust - Once a lustful thought arises, the mind is contaminated. Men and women are alike where lust is concerned. Avoid giving rise to such lustful thought.

The conditions of lust - Avoid places that encourage many opportunities for licentious acts. In those places, a simple eye contact between man and woman would draw them towards sex. It is best to avoid such places.

The methods of lust - All pornographic books and drawings, sexual caressing and touching, sex toys, sex shops, and enhancement tools and methods must be avoided.

The karma or activity of lust - Avoid all activities of licentious acts, including operating a sex-based business, which should be prohibited.

When I wrote these books, *Living this Moment in Purity, Living this Moment of Illumination*, and *The Old Man's Secret Diary* to advise the lost ones to wake up from their dreams and mend their ways while there is still time. People in general who can turn from their lustful ways will be able to live longer, cultivate their virtue, advance their aspiration, and continue to enjoy their fortune. Practitioners will be able to inspire and enlighten the world to practice truthfully, dwell in purity and freedom, and be liberated from all defilements.

Keep it up. Keep it up.

When I wrote these books, *Living this Moment in Purity*, *Living this Moment of Illumination*, and *The Old Man's Secret Diary* to advise the lost ones to wake up from their dreams and mend their ways while there is still time. People in general who can turn from their lustful ways will be able to live longer, cultivate their virtue, advance their aspiration, and continue to enjoy their fortune.

Sheng-yen Lu

16 The Crowd Who Prayed for Nectar

There is a method in Zen Buddhism on the contemplation of a phrase or question from a koan that is described like this: First, imagine that your body is affected with a severe sickness and you have died. Then contemplate your corpse being taken to a cremation ground where it is burned into a heap of ashes, which then transforms into fine dusts that are blown away by a strong wind.

Finally, imagine that there is nothing left, not even the hair and bones. At this moment, recite "Namo Amitabha Buddha" once. Immediately reflect and observe "who is chanting the Buddha's name?"

Continue doing this. Contemplate on "who is chanting the Buddha?" until you forget your body and mind. Upon hearing the sound "Li," you will become enlightened.

There is also a similar teaching in Vajrayana Buddhism which is expressed as this:

RAM - The body is set on fire. The body is burned into ashes.
YAM - The ashes are blown away by a strong gust of wind.
KAM - Everything turns into emptiness.
RAM, YAM, KAM represent fire, wind, and void.
Afterwards, light appears. Your self-nature attains buddhahood in

the luminosity of the great Vairocana Dharma Realm.

Looking at Zen and Vajrayana practices, are there any differences?

I bring this up first for a reason, as this will act as a lead into the story of this article.

During my spiritual travel, I passed the sky above a crematory. There were nine fire pits that could burn nine corpses all at once.

In the early days, the cremation grounds used wood. A hundred kati of wood was needed just to cremate one body. Nowadays, gas or electricity is used instead of wood which are much more powerful. If the cremation is carried out in the morning, by afternoon, the ashes can be collected. According to a custom known as the "four items of gold," the head and the four limbs are placed inside an urn, which is then placed inside a pagoda.

I resided in the space above the cremation ground and recited, "Be reborn in the Pure Land, and transcend birth and suffering. Namo Amitabha Buddha." At that moment, I saw sparks of astral light gathering above the cremation ground. These sparks were actually the spiritual light of beings that were cremated in the fire. But why were they gathering?

I was curious and asked, "What are you doing here?"

"We want to ask for nectar!" everyone said.

"Where do you get this nectar from?"

"Leaf Lake."

"Leaf Lake?" I got suspicious. That was my place of seclusion. That name was given by me. It was not an official name of any location and nobody should know about "Leaf Lake."

They said, "The hermit is a living buddha. The lake near his place of seclusion resembles a leaf. Thus, he called it Leaf Lake. Worldly people do not know about it but we know. Ghosts have five supernatural powers. Once the word is out it spreads around like wild fire. We want to go to him to supplicate for the nectar."

I knew what they were talking about but I kept quiet and left.

Who is the Nectar King Tathagata? He is none other than Amitabha Buddha.

Nectar and nectar dharma are the teachings about truth, taught by the Tathagata. Upon reaching the teachings, sentient beings are relieved of their defilements, similar to drinking nectar, which the teachings and practice can lead to nirvana and pure bliss.

The nectar that I produced is known as the "Water of Three HUMs" which derives from the mantra "**OM AH HUM**." It is created by writing Sanskrit syllable of "HUM" three times on the water. The spiritually charged water can purify the karmic hindrances of sentient beings. The nectar by its innate spiritual nature, is able to gather and focus the spiritual forces of the great universe. By consuming it, it can enable one to reach enlightenment, achieve purification, remove karma, and eliminate worries, spiritualizing the individual to one's highest potential.

When ghosts consume my nectar, the door of the Buddha-nature will open, allowing them to merge with their self-nature and bath in light.

When they consume my nectar, they can travel through time and space, and will not suffer from hunger in the bardo state. They will be freed from all kinds of restrictions and even be able to ascend to the heavenly realm because they have been purified.

Not only do I aspire to save the physical beings, but I also want to help the invisible beings (of the netherworld). This is what I strive for. I want to fulfill my wish to help sentient beings that are both physical and spiritual.

This nectar can enable beings in the netherworld to let go of their attachment to their ego and release them of their suffering from other attachments. By merging the mind with one's Buddha-nature, one can enter the highest level of the Western Paradise of Ultimate Bliss, where there are no bondages and only happiness.

For this reason, the Vajrayana teachings state that when birds consume water or rice transmitted by practitioners, they can be reborn into the Pure Land.

So while I was at Leaf Lake, I empowered the offering water with the proper ritual and mantra and turned it into nectar charged with the power of compassion. In all sincerity, I became one with the cosmic consciousness and our union was transformed into an energy which was beneficial to both the physical and spiritual beings.

Ever since I have been in Seattle, I have never stopped offering nectar except for a few short occasions when I arrived in Leaf Lake. To me, this is practicing generosity. This is why I offer nectar everyday. Because of this offering of the nectar, the news spread everywhere in the netherworld. By helping others, I also help myself. I don't want to place attention on my weakening health, but instead continue to offer the nectar everyday. Here is the mantra:

> **The Great Garuda**
> **Spirits in the wilderness**
> **Rakshasa and Hariti**
> **The sky is filled with elixir**
> **[transliteration: Om, mu-di, so-ha. Om, mu-di, so-ha. Om, mu-di, so-ha.]**
> **[Sanskrit: OM MUKTI SOHA. OM MUKTI SOHA. OM MUKTI SOHA.]**
> **OM AH HUM. HUM HUM HUM.**

When I offer the nectar, it is not performed by me alone. I also invoke Venerable Sariputra, who is foremost in wisdom; Venerable Maudgalyayana, who is foremost in supernatural power; Venerable Mahakasyapa, who is foremost in ascetic practice; Venerable Mahakatyayana, who is foremost in debate; Venerable Mahakausthila, who is foremost in question-and-answer; Venerable Revata, who is foremost in remaining free of error and confusion; Venerable Suddhipanthaka, who is foremost in upholding the truth of absolute reality; Venerable Nanda, who is foremost in formal comportment, Venerable Ananda, who is foremost in hearing the sutras; Venerable Rahula, who is foremost in esoteric practices and diligence; Venerable Gavampati, who is foremost in receiving the offerings of the gods; Venerable Pindola-bharadvaja, who is foremost as a field of blessings for sentient beings; Venerable Kalodayin, who is foremost in spreading the teaching; Venerable Mahakapphina, who is foremost in knowledge of astronomy; Venerable Vakula, who is foremost in longevity and Venerable Aniruddha, who is foremost in the magical ability of his divine eye. (These are the sixteen arahats who are truly great beings of dharma who manifest as sravaka, the hearer.)

They empower the nectar.

Sentient beings are worthy to receive the nectar
The netherworld since long ago knows its reputation
Now with the nectar I deliver sentient beings
Inferior beings are transformed into superior beings

The Buddhas once told me, "Lian-sheng, for the convenience of sentient beings, you must exercise Prajnaparamita, the perfection of wisdom. Through the spiritually empowered water, you offer sentient beings peace of mind, setting them free. Because of this, they attain the buddha body, his exquisite voice, purified pervading influence of moral discipline, the experience of all Dharma flavors, a gentle heart, a purified mind, and the blessings of receiving the Dharma discourses. This is the equanimity of the Tathagata. Through these methods, you save all sentient beings. It is the pure dharma of thusness and therefore, you can be named the Supreme Nectar King."

I felt ashamed and undeserving of the praise.

One day while I was offering the nectar, I tossed it into the air where a group of beings were waiting to receive it.

I heard someone said, "Isn't that the spiritual traveler whom we saw in the space above the cremation fire?" Obviously someone had recognized me.

"It was him indeed!"

One of them said, "This sage looks as ordinary as any mortal beings."

"Never judge by appearance, just like you can't measure sea water by the gallon."

"It is very difficult to find a practitioner who offers real nectar."

"All accomplished practitioners have already gone into seclusion."

One of the spirits who understood the Buddhadharma said, "Maudgalyayana was clubbed to death by heretics. Bodhidharma also retreated to the cave, where he meditated facing a wall for nine years in Song Mountain. Living Buddha Ji Gong was kicked out of the Ling Yin Temple. The Sixth Patriarch Huineng hid with a group of hunters [for fifteen years]. When one is a sage, it is impossible to avoid such tests and trials."

"Why does this happen?" asked a spirit.

"How can mortal eyes recognize a true sage!" said another.

"Some people do not know anything, but they pretend that they do," someone added.

These crowds came for the nectar. There were hundreds and thousands of spirits. While it is true that spirit (bardo) and the physical body are different, the difference is that the physical body is only a shell.

All the spirits left except for an old man who was kneeling. I was surprised.

"Haven't you already received the nectar?"

The old man cried, "I wanted to get some for my master too."

"I only give to those who are present," I said.

"He couldn't come. He jumped off a building and killed himself. He cannot move. His mouth is disfigured and his four limbs are broken.

He is……"

I was shocked. The guy who killed himself was a famous personality. What a pity! I gave the old man some more nectar, and he thanked me and left.

Here is a verse:

> **Death by suicide makes it difficult for a person to rise again**
> **No one can possibly gain rebirth by suicide**
> **Nectar sprinkled over the body washes away all impurities**
> **With hope that in one's next life one realizes buddhahood**

Sentient beings are worthy to receive the nectar
The netherworld since long ago knows its reputation
Now with the nectar I deliver sentient beings
Inferior beings are transformed into superior beings

Sheng-yen Lu

17 The Languages of the Heavens

I crossed path with someone who was also traveling spiritually. He started talking to me but his voice sounded very peculiar yet had a softer tone to it. I listened attentively and realized that he was speaking in some foreign tongue. After a while, I began to understand what he was saying.

He said, "Puxi! Puxi!" (It meant "hi.")

"Ji! Ji!" (How are you?) he continued.

I asked, "Where are you from?"

He replied, "The Yama Deva Realm."

I immediately understood that he was a celestial being from the Kamadhatu Realm (the realm of desire). In this realm, there is desire for sex and food. Spanning across this realm of desire are the six heavens in the upper region, the middle region of the four continents where humans and animals reside, right down to the Avici hell.

The languages found in the realm of desire are extremely complex. Human languages alone already include Chinese, American, French, German, Russian, Japanese, Arabic, Brazilian and Mexican among others. Every country in the world has its own set of languages and dialects. Just imagine the amount of languages contained in the realm of desire. Their languages are simply uncountable, indescribable, for they are innumerable.

To my knowledge, there are different languages in the animal realm, the hell realm, and the hungry ghost realm. The languages that are most audibly disgusting are the languages of the asura realm, which literally come across like sounds heard on a killing field, strikingly hard, just like the screeching sound of a rock that is struck against metal.

At the heavenly level of the four deva-kings and above, the languages in these heavenly realms are vastly diverse. While some languages are similar, others are different. From the realm of desire to the first dhyana heaven including the Heaven of the Followers of Brahma, Heaven of the Assistants of Brahma, the Heaven of the Great Brahma, there are languages in existence. Beginning from the second dhyana heaven, language is used less. I classify languages in the heaven into three categories, which are:

1. Language
2. Light
3. Consciousness

In the spiritual world, the lower realms use words to communicate. In the middle realms, beings communicate by pure light and at the higher realms, beings only express themselves through consciousness. Only beings who can intuit the minds of others or the Buddha would understand this. Otherwise, it is confusing.

Beings in the Yama Heaven speak in a very gentle and soft voice, and it is not sharp.

The Yama Deva said to me, "Beings with heavy resentment have a coarse voice. Beings with great compassion speak with a gentle voice. These are their natural characteristics and innate ability. Truly accomplished beings do not use language, for rely on light, or consciousness for communication. In fact, they don't need to say anything or rely on anything, except by transmission from mind to mind."

I replied, "No wonder the Tathagata has three modes of discourses, which are to give discourse out of the fullness of his nature, to give discourse adapting truth to the capacity of his hearers, and to give discourse combining the two approaches. The Tathagata can voluntary express his attainment of the absolute Dharma. The Buddha can expound all kinds of Dharma tailoring to sentient beings of varying capacities. The Buddha can also express the Dharma according to his will or the needs of others, expressing hundreds and thousands of dharmas in one voice to all sentient beings."

The Yama Deva said, "Though the Buddha had expounded eighty-four thousand dharmas to worldly beings, the spiritual realization that he had attained could not be expressed in words. All of the discourses given by him had always existed as it is, and were neither created by the Buddha nor did they come into existence after he had expounded on them. Thus, it was just like nothing had been said. Therefore, the Buddha remarked that he had not uttered a single word of Dharma."

I nodded and agreed, "Yes, yes."

There were three more travellers.

One said, "Xiaoxiao."

Another said, "Susu."

The third person said, "Fufu."

The Yama Deva said, "Living Buddha Lian-sheng, Sheng-yen Lu, I don't understand their language. What kind of language are they speaking?"

I replied, "They are tree deities."

The tree deities nodded.

The Yama Deva was filled with admiration for my extensive knowledge.

The three tree deities continued their conversation with me.

The Yama Deva asked me what they were saying and I replied,

"They have just cooked some noodles and wanted to invite both of us to have some."

I never would have imagined that the Yama Deva's favourite food were noodles. During his incarnation on earth as a practitioner, the Yama Deva was particularly fond of noodles. Having heard about the invitation, the Yama Deva was so thrilled and together we traveled to the home of the tree deities.

There were five bowls of hot noodles readily served.

The Yama Deva was so hungry that he picked up the chopsticks and wanted to eat right away.

I tuned into my divine vision and immediately stopped him.

The Yama Deva asked, "Why can't I eat it?"

"Take a closer look to see what kind of noodles they are."

The Yama Deva looked at the noodles with his divine vision and he was taken aback.

"These are not noodles. These are earthworms!"

I concurred, "They are earthworms indeed."

The Yama Deva was going to reprimand the tree deities right away but I said, "Don't blame them. Perception is shifted from realm to realm. According to the tree deities, earthworms are considered noodles to them. There are marked differences in the perceptions between higher and lower level beings. Please do not be angry."

I cited an example of a glass of water.

People see the glass of water as a glass of water.

Hungry ghost see the glass of water as a ball of fire.

The ghosts in the hell realm see the glass of water as a glass of blood.

The Buddha sees the glass of water as a glass filled with eighty-four thousand worms.

I said, "Within the three realms, there are sex and food in the realm of desire. There is no sex and food in the realm of form but there is the appearance of pure light. There is only consciousness in the realm of the formless. Therefore, sentient beings in the realm of desire use their mouths to speak. Beings use the color of light as language in the realm of form. Consciousness is the language used in the realm of the formless. If the Yama Deva criticized the noodles of the tree deities, then he was being attached to his own biased view. After all, these earthworms were actually noodles to them and they were delicacies for the tree deities!"

They invited us for noodles, and we should be thankful.

I have been thinking about a question all along. Cultivation starts from the beginner's level towards the higher levels. This is the way to remove karmic hindrances, and to enhance good fortune and wisdom. But, nowadays, we live in a world where human beings consume all kinds of meat for their enjoyment. Is this considered a high level culture or a low-level lifestyle?

In human warfare, people kill people. Is this a high-level or low-level state? What kind of religion would advocate this?

In the spiritual world, the lower realms use words to communicate. In the middle realms, beings communicate by pure light and at the higher realms, beings only express themselves through consciousness. Only beings who can intuit the minds of others or the Buddha would understand this. Otherwise, it is confusing.

Sheng-yen Lu

18 Traveling in the Blood Spilled Kingdom

I came to a barren land and looked around. This place was red everywhere beyond the horizon. The whole space and ground were red. Upon taking a closer look, I saw that it was actually blood flowing and covering the earth and I was stunned. I smelled thick pungent blood and the stench was really unbearable. In this wilderness, there were also "human habitats" inhabited by beings who were beheaded, or found with mangled torsos, amputated hands, and legs all dripping with blood.

The "human habitats" were further subdivided into clans. Every ethnic group had its own units, whose populations were countless. The whole region was filled with beings that were bleeding profusely. How dreadful! How agonizing!

Here is a verse:

> **Skin wrapped over fat and blood**
> **Rotten flesh and bone make a thick broth**
> **Oozing a mix of pus and blood**
> **Since ancient times, battles have always been fought**

These clans were formed from those who were killed in battle, whose souls later grouped together, forming one clan after another that appeared in countless numbers. They all cried out with grief and hatred. Even heaven and earth were suffused in a bloody red. How pitiful! How sad!

When I came to a certain region, I saw a thin layer of "wisdom light" enveloping a certain clan and I was amazed.

I told myself, "So strange to see the presence of wisdom light in this place!"

As I entered into this shield of wisdom light, I met an elderly man who had a crippled leg and blood was seen dripping from its wound. I asked him, "What kind of place is this?"

He answered, "Blood Spilled Kingdom."

"Why does a clan in the Blood Spilled Kingdom shielded in the wisdom light?"

"By the grace and power of the Buddha, our clan is somewhat different from others because we are the Shakya clan that perished long ago."

"Oh!" I was astounded by the revelation.

"The Shakya clan is still residing in the Blood Spilled Kingdom?" I asked.

The old man explained, "Since ancient times, all kingdoms and clans that were annihilated had settled in the Blood Spilled Kingdom."

I believe Buddhists are familiar with the event of the Shakya clan being annihilated.

Buddhists who are fully ordained would change their last name to "Shakya" [in Chinese], in reference to this verse stated in *the Agama Sutras*:

> **Just as the four rivers that enter the sea**
> **Can no longer retain their identities**
> **When the four castes are ordained**

All shall be known by the Shakya name

Shakyamuni (meaning "kind, capable, tranquil and silent") was the prince of Kapilavastu Kingdom in ancient India [modern day Nepal]. His father was King Suddhodana and his mother was Queen Maya. "Shakya" is the name of their clan. During that time, King Prasenajit of Kosala Kingdom made a marriage proposal to the Shakya clan.

However, the Shakyans felt that their clan was far superior and they did not want to marry their princess to the King Prasenajit. It was unwise though to refuse him because he had a very strong military presence.

Subsequently, a Shakya noble named Mahanama thought of an idea to dress up one of his maid servants, named Mallika, as the princess and married her to the king instead. Later on, Mallika had a son named Prince Virudhaka.

When Prince Virudhaka was eight years old he was sent to Kapilavastu to learn archery by the order of his father, King Prasenajit. Once he saw a platform built for Buddha's discourse, he wondered into it. When the Shakyans learned about it, they believed that their holy place had been polluted by the son of a slave. To cleanse the place, they dug out seven feet of dirt and covered the place with fresh soil. (Caste discrimination was very serious in ancient India.)

When Prince Virudhaka found out about this, he was deeply humiliated and vowed, "When I become king, I will wipe out the entire Shakya clan and the Kapilavastu Kingdom."

He annihilated the Shakya clan eventually.

The Buddha had tried to save the Shakya clan and persuaded King Virudhaka many times to withdraw his army. But the Shakya clan was eventually wiped out due to the ripening of karma.

There was another story that describes King Virudhaka's past life as a big fish. The Shakya people caught this fish and the whole village ate it, except for a little boy. Out of curiosity, however, the little boy hit the head of the fish three times. This child was later reborn as Shakyamuni Buddha. Because the Buddha had hit the fish's head three times in his past life, he suffered migraine during his lifetime. (In the *Ekottaragama Sutra* or *Increase by One Agama Sutras* Volume 26, Chapter on Equal View, the Buddha was recorded as having a migraine.)

The pain of the headache is like being squashed by a boulder As though the head was toppled by Mount Meru

Oh what a pain this is!

Buddhism talks about the retribution of cause and effect. There are three kinds of retribution.

Present life's retribution refers to retribution in this life for one's deeds.

Life's retribution refers to deeds done in this life that produce results in the next life.

Future life's retribution refers to deeds done in this life but the retributions are received in subsequent lives. (This does not mean that retribution will not happen, but it will happen when the time is ripe.)

Even the great enlightened Buddha could not save his own kingdom, clan, and brothers, due to the cause and effect of "fixed karma." One must bear the retribution of deeds done in the past. Even the enlightened Buddha himself had to bear the fruit of karma. The retribution of cause and effect is exact in every way.

I asked the old man, "Why does your clan enjoy the presence of wisdom light?"

He replied, "It's back to cause and effect. The Buddha was from the Shakya clan. Because he empathized with the suffering people in the Blood Spilled Kingdom, he came to this place and radiated the wisdom light that he had cultivated and attained to shield and protect the clan. Whenever the clansmen complain about heavy bleeding, the bleeding will stop. When crops wither they will be revived. When irrigation runs dry, water will flow again. When there is a drought, the rain will shower. When there are floods, the flood waters will recede. The Buddha also made his sacrifice and genuinely tried to save our clan. He tried with utmost effort to minimize the suffering that our people received in the Blood Spilled Kingdom."

"Then why didn't the Buddha save all the Shakya clansmen by delivering them to the Pure Land of Ultimate Bliss?"

The old man laughed and said, "Didn't you know that a person is responsible for his own karma?"

"Indeed," I nodded.

He said, "The Buddha only teaches the method of cultivation. To attain results, one actually has to cultivate."

I asked, "May I ask who you are?"

In turn, he asked me, "Who are you really?"

He disappeared in the gust of the wind.

Even the great enlightened Buddha could not save his own kingdom, clan, and brothers, due to the cause and effect of "fixed karma." One must bear the retribution of deeds done in the past. Even the enlightened the Buddha himself had to bear the fruit of karma. The retribution of cause and effect is exact in every way.

Sheng-yen Lu

19 Protectors inside the Pores

I believe that my practice is the "right practice."
Buddhism developed into Hinayana, Mahayana, and Vajrayana (the Diamond Vehicle). Then there were further divisions leading to the Vinaya School (monastic discipline), Abhidharma School, Satyasiddhi School, Three Sastra School, Tiantai School, Huayan or Avatamsaka School, Cien School (also known as Dharmalaksana School or Faxiang School), Zen School, Vajrayana School, and the Pure Land School, among others.

However, in my view, their teachings are differentiated solely on the Buddha's deliverance of sentient beings with different spiritual capacities. All in all they are the best spiritual vessels for crossing the ocean of life and death, and reaching the shore of nirvana.

I practice the Vajrayana teachings along with the Pure Land practices, and these are the right practices.

The differences between teachings, in my view, can be summed up as: A matter of opinions and perspectives.

Here are some examples:

Keeping the Five Precepts - [rebirth in the] human realm.

Performing the Ten Good Deeds - [rebirth in the] heaven realm.

Practicing the Four Foundations of Mindfulness - [cultivating in the] path of liberation.

Practicing the Ten Perfections - [entering the] bodhisattva path.

Perfect and Wondrous Enlightenment - [attainment of] buddhahood.

I possess the right knowledge, right thought, right writing, right action, right dharma obligation, right diligence, right mind, and right meditation. I do practice the right dharma!

I practice discipline, and I am pure and prudent in my actions. I practice the samadhi of stabilizing the mind. I cultivate wisdom, such as the wisdom of liberation, and the wisdom of enlightenment.

I know the right dharma is the Truth of the Universe. Pseudo teachings have deviated from the Universal Truth, and "evil practices" rely on the power of the elemental spirit world. Those practices are considered the dark art.

(I have noticed many religious groups today claim that they are practicing the right dharma, but unknowingly they are practicing sorcery in the name of the right dharma. To practice the right dharma, one has to practice the Eightfold Noble Path.)

We are referring to teachings that speak of thusness, prajna, consciousness-only, mind seal, omniscience, primordial wisdom, nirvana and the other shore. These teachings are the sutras that are uphold and protected by all buddhas. They are the secret treasure dharma of all buddhas, and they represent the five periods of the Buddha's teachings that guide one to attaining enlightenment in most direct way.

Thus:
> Even a single pore delivers the message whose reality, unhidden, spans the dharma realm.

Once, during a spiritual travel, I arrived at a realm of the elementals where I saw a person performing dark sorcery. He was seated high up on his throne and apparently within his pores were hidden eighty-four thousand elemental spirits, whose forms were golden in color.

The elemental spirits shape-shifted into the appearance of Tathagatas and flew into the space.

In the centre was seated Vairocana who was surrounded by thousands of buddhas, and countless bodhisattvas and lotus flowers emerging spontaneously.

Then, mountains, rivers and lands of the ten directions were transformed into places resembling the Buddha Pure Lands, complete with the Seven Treasures. Light illuminated all corners, and adding to its incredibly beautiful celestial realms were magnificent palaces of exquisite beauty.

The individual who performed the evil sorcery proclaimed that he had attained unexcelled complete perfect enlightenment, and he was expounding passages from the sutras as he sat sternly on the dharma throne. Below him, a huge audience was in attendance, completely mesmerized by his spiritual power.

His hand radiated lights towards the crowns of his believers, empowering them as their heads glowed in his lights. They bowed to him.

The evil sorcerer boasted about his extraordinary spiritual power, proclaiming his ability to enter a fire and escape through it, to submerge in water and not drown, to dwell in space, and to pass through mountains and walls without obstruction.

The evil sorcerer could communicate with the elemental spirits, read the past lives of people, and was very accurate in his readings. People were bewitched and they believed him. Even monks and nuns bowed to him and became his students.

He slandered other ordained masters, and slandered the teachings of Mahayana, Hinayana and Vajrayana. He praised himself and defamed others, proclaiming that he was the only one in the world who had attained the supreme way and that all other practices were evil.

It was unnerving to encounter such an individual in my spiritual travel. What appeared to be eighty-four thousand elemental spirits from his pores had actually transformed themselves into eighty-four thousand Tathagatas. That alone was frightening.

When I met such a person, I knew that the forces of demonic spirits and the mighty elemental spirits were extremely strong in their interference with the practitioners. It was simply terrible.

Therefore the ancients had uttered these words, "It is better not to be enlightened for a thousand days than to be trapped by mara in a moment of foolishness."

"As virtue rises one foot, vice rises ten."

"Whatever the level of one's spiritual attainment is, it is matched by the mara king."

When I saw that scenario, I was extremely shocked and wanted to hurry away, as I had no intention to stay any longer in the elemental spirit world. This realm of evil sorcery would only be temporary and we must not indulge in it.

As I was about to leave, the evil sorcerer noticed me and said, "Look, that is Living Buddha Lian-sheng, Sheng-yen Lu! He wants to run away and dares not meet me, the holy one. I was going to challenge him but he just ran away. Apparently he had not attained buddhahood and gained the Buddha's mind, and he is nothing but a practitioner satisfied with inferior teachings."

The evil sorcerer uttered, "Living Buddha Lian-sheng, Sheng-yen Lu is actually possessed by the demons. He is really no big deal! He is just a heretic."

When the crowd heard this, they applauded in agreement.

Due to the countless unfortunate circumstances and events that I have encountered in this life, I no longer harbour resentment towards anyone and I am able to focus my mind on the practice of the right dharma and remain immovable. This state is called the Ground of Tolerance.

I have attained the level of tolerance known as "patience through seeing all phenomena as uncreated," as well as the tolerance of the "seven virtuous stages." This is the wisdom of tolerance and it is as strong as a vajra.

I have endured all different kinds of humiliation and practiced the paramita of tolerance.

I have practiced the "transcendental dharma of wuwei [unconditioned existence]" which includes the transcendence of emptiness, the transcendence by means of destruction of defilements through the wisdom of awakening, the transcendence of non-analytical cessation, the transcendence achieved by being unmoved by pleasure or pain, the transcendence through cessation of sensation of perception, and the transcendence of thusness.

I ignored the evil sorcerer.

However, he tried to provoke me and said, "Living Buddha Liansheng, Sheng-yen Lu is useless. He is not a man!"

"He follows the unorthodox path of Buddhism. He should come and seek refuge in me as his master but if he did, I would not accept him nor would I take him as my student's student. We don't want anything to do with this kind of low life."

"So he thinks he is a living buddha. He might as well be called a living ape!"

They laughed in mockery.

Hidden within the pores of the evil sorcerer were eighty-four thousand animal elemental spirits. They all emerged and through my divine eye, I saw spirits of foxes, ogres, tigers, elephants, cows, snakes, spiders, lions, toads, turtles, and so forth. However, in the eyes of the mundane, they were seen as thousands of buddhas because the spirits had disguised themselves as such. I was surrounded by all of them.

The animal elemental spirits breathed out poisonous mist and toxic rays in an attempt to kill me. Though I wanted to run away, there was nowhere to go.

These spirits were corrupted with greed, filled with hatred and intolerance, lustful in every sexual opportunity, egotistical, irrational, indoctrinated with evil views, and were skeptical of the right dharma.

They opened their mouths widely, wanting to devour me.

Not only was the sorcerer's body embedded with numerous evil spirits in his pores, but his disciples were also possessed by these elemental spirits. (They were jumping and hopping around everywhere.)

I couldn't bear to watch the scene unfold but I remained there waiting to be killed. I blamed myself for coming to this place and getting murdered.

I recited this poem:

> **Traveling spiritually, where darkness glooms and autumn waters run cold**
> **All alone, I moved through dense forest**
> **Shocked to discover the face of truth in this world**
> **My only thought is to gain rebirth in the Western Pure Land**

My tears flowed as I thought about the difficult life I led at Leaf Lake, where my only solace in all my cultivation life was carrying out meditation and spiritual traveling. To think that I was going to be chewed by these evil spirits, where my spirit would suffer a fate of complete annihilation in form and essence was most distressing and pathetic.

I started crying at the most critical time; my hair stood on its end while my pores enlarged, through which emerged numerous dharma protectors. I believed there were eighty-four thousands of them!

These protectors emitted black, green, red, blue, yellow, and golden light in accordance to the color of their appearances. They all came out from my pores.

Even the "Smiling Face Ghost King" in my thumb appeared and laughed.

The dharma protectors told me, "Don't be afraid, we are here!"

I asked, "Where are all of you residing normally?"

"Inside your eighty-four thousand pores."

"Who else reside in my pores?"

"Dharma Protector Skanda and Sangharama, among others."

I asked, "What about Yamantaka?" (This was my great protector.)

"Chant his mantra!"

I chanted,

"[transliteration: Om, dzu-lee, kah-lah, roo-pah, hum-kan, so-ha] [Sanskrit: OM STRIH KALARUPA HUM KHAM SOHA]."

Instantly, Yamantaka appeared as a giant with multiple hands and feet. He had a bull's head with wrathful eyes, whose mouth opened widely to reveal his canine teeth and a protruding tongue. He growled and uttered the words "**HUM, HUM, HUM**," whose sound trembled like thunder. He twirled and emitted strong powerful blue rays.

When the elemental spirits saw this, they were scared to death and shrunk into tiny worms.

Yamantaka had no mercy. He inhaled a gulp of air and with the sound "[**transliteration: Hum, zha-zha.**] [**Sanskrit: HUM PHAT**]."

He swallowed all the little worms.

The evil sorcerer saw this and hid under his seat, trembling all over.

All of his followers froze and fled in all directions. Yamantaka wanted to step on them but I felt compassion for them and said, "Cultivation is no easy feat. These beings do have souls except that they had followed the wrong master. They did not do any bad deeds such as killing or hurting people, or committing harmful actions. So long as they sincerely repent, please let them go."

Yamantaka lifted his leg, but he did not tramp on them. He let them off the hook.

I said, "The Buddhadharma is boundless. One must repent and be saved. Practice with sincerity, take refuge in the right dharma, and do not follow evil spirits. Get rid of the three poisons and five desires, and practice diligently. Through these methods, your merits will grow. Follow the right dharma and cultivate!"

When I finished speaking, I left.

The eighty-four thousand protectors retreated back into my pores. I realized that there were so many protectors looking after me. They have the following responsibilities:

1. They protect the life of the true practitioner who upholds and practices the right dharma.
2. They protect the true practitioner who follows the right dharma from misfortune.
3. They prevent harm inflicted upon the true practitioner by evil spirits in times of need.
4. They offer guidance to the true practitioner.
5. As the true practitioner advances spiritually, the dharma protector responsible for him shall advance concurrently.
6. The level of merit of the dharma protector also depends on the progress of the practitioner.
7. Together they attain the fruition of buddhahood and bodhisattvahood.

20 Lingering around a Fetus

Once I met a kindhearted lady where I immediately experienced a burst of emotion, suggesting that she and I were connected in affinity. I became uncontrollably sad.

She was pregnant with a baby boy, and this boy had lots of wisdom and courage. In the future, he would have a good upbringing and would enjoy great fame.

Her parents were kind and they were Buddhists. Furthermore, her husband was warm, courteous and well educated, and he was from a wealthy and noble family.

She was kind and compassionate, and was always willing to help the poor and do charitable acts. She also chanted the Buddha's name earnestly. Her heart was pure and kind.

I studied her ancestors and saw that they were all famous people, scholars, and specialists who were loyal descendents from rare families of a high caliber. No wonder I felt so emotional without cause.

Honestly, the retreat I had at Leaf Lake was different from those I had in the past. Time really has no mercy on those who rarely fell sick, and in my case, I had enjoyed a healthy life for a good sixty years. However, at Leaf Lake, I began to fall ill.

When I investigated my illnesses, I realized that they were the results of karmic hindrances which were cyclical in nature, that were not necessarily created in this life but were created in previous lives due to one's misconduct. While I was in retreat at Leaf Lake, I was confronted by the surfacing of these past karmas. (As long as you are human, you will have karma.)

I grieved and said, "The good fortune is gone and now the karmic hindrances are appearing."

Although years of practice have led to my attainment of self-realization, where I am aware of my karmic consequences from previous lives, I am still subjected to cyclical karma that has not yet been fully eradicated. In fact, my illnesses were the result of working out these lingering karmas. Becoming old and falling ill completely adhere to the law of nature in the material world.

When I was young and healthy, I seldom fell sick. In fact, I never knew what the pain of sickness felt like but now that I had tasted it, I realized how dreadful it really was. During my retreat, I endured the pain and suffered, and while enduring its torment, I focused my mind on the Four Foundations of Mindfulness which are:

Contemplating on the impurity of the body.
Contemplating on the suffering of emotions.
Contemplating on the impermanence of mind.
Contemplating on the fact that all things are devoid of inherent existence.

The sufferings continued on and on.

When I cried out in pain, the buddhas and bodhisattvas also knew about it.

Torn between being alive and dead, I began to journey in order to get away from the pain that was inflicting my body. Right now, I had no desires and I didn't ask for anything. Everything in the world is just a dream. If we can't even hold on to our body, then what more is there to say about our skin and hair?

I am an enlightened person. Should I leave my body, I would instantly see the natural beauty of the original state, and I could return to the Maha Twin Lotus Ponds of the Western Paradise of Ultimate Bliss. I am my own buddha. There is no doubt about this.

However, the moment I ended my journey and returned to my body, the suffering resumed. No one is free from old age and sickness. There is nothing to fear about death. The only thing that anyone should be afraid of is old age and sickness.

Although I have totally abandoned the attachment to all things, the condition of my body remains. After all, our physical body is shaped by our karma and time. I always thought that I was physically strong, and never would've guessed that my seemingly indestructible body would now be breaking down.

I thought of a verse by Samantabhadra Bodhisattva:

> **The day has gone by**
> **And life has come to an end for the day**
> **Like fish that live in shallow water**
> **What joy is there in this**

Another verse:

> **Lost, we have forgotten our lotus within this fire**
> **As I remain in retreat how long must I suffer these illnesses**
> **When pain is felt in the body there is nowhere I can avoid it**
> **My only solace is to travel spiritually to where the Buddha is**

One more verse:

> **While we proclaim old age and sickness as hindrances**
> **It is only until one faces old age and sickness that we learn to give up our attachments**

This is the opportune time where we accumulate merit and virtue
Such merit and virtue would not have arisen through deep-seated attachments

The Buddha said, "Illness, old age, the eight kinds of suffering, and all other kinds of suffering are good because they create the need for one to cultivate in order to leave 'the house of fire' [samsara]. If one is attached to emotional love and desire, rebirth in the Pure Land would not be easy."

I was babbling too much right now, mainly because I was overwhelmed by an unexplainable bout of emotion. Suddenly I felt like abandoning my body and entering into the fetus of that lady to take up a new body. This Vajrayana method is known as drongjuk or forceful projection into a body.

In time I would be an incarnated living buddha that has returned to save sentient beings. For this reason I want to be reincarnated because this would fulfill my solemn vow of succoring all beings in all lifetimes. I would not leave this life, solely out of despair.

The ability to determine one's reincarnation from one lifetime to another is a unique characteristic of a rinpoche (living buddha) and this is a major reason why Buddhism has survived. This is the truth behind the cycle of reincarnation in the universe. The Vajrayana teachings being transmitted and received through the lineage reveal the wisdom about the original nature (Buddha-nature) that remains unchanged, so long as it is not eroded by time, tempted by material wants or drowned by desires.

As a practitioner whose wisdom is inherently complete, I am able to tap into this wisdom to teach and propagate the right dharma and save sentient beings when the affinity ripens. I will be able to ascend the dharma throne and help those who have lost touch with their original nature. This is my responsibility.

I hesitated and wondered back and forth, pondering if I should incarnate into a new body, as virtuous women do not come by often or perhaps it would be a better idea to gain rebirth in the Maha Twin Lotus Ponds.

I was overwhelmed by the problem of whether I should continue to live at Leaf Lake and if so, how long could I survive? My life in solitary retreat is concerned with writing and practicing the dharma. That is my life. I would become older and sicker and in the end, I would have to abandon my body anyway.

What hope did I need to keep while living at Leaf Lake?

Was there anything that I still couldn't let go of?

Were there any wishes that I had not fulfilled yet?

By pondering these questions, it meant that I had already let go of everything. I was already accustomed to my daily life here and I could continue to live like this, without ever leaving Leaf Lake, until the day I die. Right now, I was only waiting for all the buddhas and deities to tell me when I could "well-depart!"

This could be described as:

> **The boundless ocean of samsara is really emptiness itself**
> **Within the ocean emerges the primordial lotus flower palace**
> **Surrounding life and death is the Pure Land**
> **Within this Pure Land one finds the countenance of Amitabha himself**

Should I wait to "be well-departed and be reborn" into the Pure Land, where I shall meet Amitabha Buddha and all virtuous people?

Or should I enter the fetus of this fine lady?

If I did, I would grow up to be an intelligent boy. I would grow up in an affluent family, go to school, get a job, marry, work hard my entire life and suffer until I am old.

Imprinted in my subconscious is my identity as "Living Buddha

Sheng-yen Lu."

However, there is a possibility that after I am born, the surrounding environment would change my mind. After all, bodhisattvas can become "lost in delusion between lifetimes." Could it be possible that I will be lost on the journey and not be able to recall my original identity?

Will I still have the ability to communicate with spirits?

Will I be blessed with a unique talent like a genius? Will I be well-versed in the Tripitaka and the twelve divisions of the Mahayana canon? In my new rebirth, will I innately know the right Dharma and practice them truthfully? Will I be able to save sentient beings? Will I gradually lose my original abilities? Will my Buddha-nature appear?

I feared that once I took rebirth, I would become an ordinary person again such as being a wealthy managing director of a large company or someone in high office in the government.

Will I still be Living Buddha Lian-Sheng?

My aim of being reborn is to practice the dharma to become a monk and save sentient beings, which is the true meaning of life. It is a perfect reason to be able to give of one's service to spread religious teachings to the world and benefit all sentient beings.

Practicing the dharma allows one to understand the Truths of the Universe, which are:

    Impermanence.

    Non-self.

    Nirvana.

I want to teach people the "Absolute Truth," which is the pure mind of self-nature of all beings. I would transmit the teachings on Dharmakaya, Dharma-nature, Tathagatagarbha, and True Buddha. Will I able to serve my spiritual purpose in the respective cause and condition amidst all appearances of arising and ceasing?

I pondered again and again and without further hesitation, I was going to rush into the fetus, thus ending my present physical life. Finally, without giving it any more thought, my consciousness as soul shrunk and rushed towards the lady's navel.

Just then I heard a voice from the sky shout out, "Lian-sheng, don't be irrational. Stop! Stop! You can't do that! You mustn't do that!"

I lifted my head to look.

It was none other than the Golden Mother of the Jade Pond herself who was adorned with a phoenix crown on her head; her left hand was holding a celestial peach while her right hand held a whisk.

Golden Mother asked, "Why are you entering this fetus?"

Tears flowed down my cheeks and I answered, "To go on living does not necessarily guarantee happiness, and I have no worries concerning death. I am thinking of leaving this body!"

Golden Mother asked, "Do you know what kind of fetus this is?"

"It is the fetus of a kindhearted lady."

Golden Mother replied, "Indeed, it is the fetus of a kind lady. You're right. In fact, it is a human fetus of royal status as the Purple or Emperor Star shines over it, and not a fetus meant for a dharma king. When you enter this fetus, you will live in a luxurious mansion and enjoy every good food. You will have chauffeurs to take you everywhere and servants to serve you. You will be born as a prince and rule as a king in the future."

"Is this so?" I was astonished

"Once you become a king and rule over your people, you will always be busy dealing with all sorts of matters. You will be drained. Though you will have lots of wealth and fortune, it will be impossible for you to resume your cultivation. In your next life, you will abandon the life of a monk, and get to taste a lifetime of wealth and fortune, but you will not have your own time. In the end, you shall experience riches and good fortune to the highest degree and in return, all of your buddha wisdom will vanish in that lifetime."

"Oh!" I gasped.

"Do you still want to enter this fetus?"

I backed out and said, "No, not anymore."

I asked Golden Mother, "When will life at Leaf Lake end?"

Golden Mother said, "Here, you have abandoned the respectful title of Living Buddha Lian-sheng so you can have a taste of void and emptiness. Don't you feel liberated in your spiritual travel and in your wisdom? Without deceit, fear, or ego, everything is spontaneous and natural. You left a world tainted with jealousy, hatred and craftiness to embrace nature. This should be a happy thing for you."

"I have illnesses."

Golden Mother responded, "Illnesses represent bodhi [awakening]."

"When will I leave this world?"

Golden Mother replied, "You will know when the time comes."

Golden Mother took me to a place and said, "I will let you take a peak at your students whom you miss so dearly. This student is the one that you have missed the most."

The moment I saw him, I gasped and felt disheartened. The student that I missed had changed.

I saw him chopping up the statue of Padmakumara into pieces, replacing the picture of Living Buddha Lian-sheng, Sheng-yen Lu, with that of another ordained monk.

He removed all the Vajrayana statues that were originally on the shrine.

He listened to others and stopped practicing the True Buddha Tantra. He burned the refuge certificate. His teacher was no longer Living Buddha Lian-sheng, Sheng-yen Lu as he had a new teacher now. In the past, I taught him earnestly and tirelessly, believing that he would be a spiritually strong person. The buddha wisdom of the Tathagata is never meant for the weak. Because of this, I was denounced by others. The person that I entrusted could not even pass the tests and trials of life. He was a weak person that did not have pure faith. Instead, he was emotional and full of suspicion, fear, and hypocrisy.

He has changed. The heart is indeed fickle.

He left with another dharma teacher. In this society, dharma teachers are a dime a dozen, each with his own special set of teachings. Who can distinguish the right dharma from the heretical teachings as well as the evil practices? He viewed me as a "heretical Buddhist master" and viewed his present teacher as an icon of right dharma. I observed his heart and found it has deteriorated and corrupted. He had affected other followers of True Buddha School and led them away. These followers had become vulnerable.

I used to be a courageous practitioner that had forged great will power, but when I saw that this student whom I missed dearly had changed, I could not control the pain within as the matter weighed on me so heavily that it almost broke me. So much so that I had wanted to discontinue the work of liberating others. Golden Mother consoled me, saying that good students remained in abundance.

Golden Mother uttered the words, "Be spontaneous and natural," and "go with the flow." She advised, "Be at home wherever you are. All problems shall disappear and all burdens shall cease to exist."

I used to be a courageous practitioner that had forged great will power, but when I saw that this student whom I missed dearly had changed, I could not control the pain within as the matter weighed on me so heavily that it almost broke me.

Sheng-yen Lu

21 The Ecstasy Addicts in Space

I saw a group of bardo spirits who gathered in space. They appeared to be drifting aimlessly and they didn't show any sign of intelligence, as they were unable to recognize the state of their condition.

All they could do was shaking their heads, having no ability to judge their surroundings. They were completely confused and lost in the vastness of space. I called these people the "Ecstasy Addicts."

I know of the existence of ecstasy addicts in the human world. Who are these addicts?

1. They habitually pursue a false sense of happiness.
2. They take the ecstasy pills.
3. They act and react as they wish.
4. They are unrealistic in their goals, and impractical in their ways.
5. They love crowds and parties.

I feel that these people have not yet experienced adversity and trials of life. They have never undergone any transformation in their mental state, nor done any form of cultivation. They don't know the significance of being alive, and have little idea what death is all about. They only indulge themselves in seeking superficial happiness and excitement.

Today's youth has degenerated and they are confused. There is no one to guide them. Their lives are simply wasted away. They drift with the mass and in time, they study, start and build their careers, get married, raise children, age, fall ill, and eventually die.

These are the stages of a person's life. Most people generally live such predictable life. Because of this, young people such as the "ecstasy addicts" feel that life is meaningless so they seek sensual pleasure and excitement.

I spoke to someone among the ecstasy addicts in space and asked, "What are you doing here?"

He answered, "I don't know."

"Why are you gathering here?"

"Bored I guess."

"Do you know what the mind is?"

"What is the mind?"

"Where is your body?"

"It has disappeared."

"Do you know how to purify, transform, and deliver yourselves?"

"No, we don't."

I had nothing further to ask. It would have been a waste of breath. These addicts were anything but holy.

They only know one thing in their lives, and that is physical desire and pleasure. They have never known about the nature of the mind nor their inner state of realization. They have never encountered any opportunity to study the Dharma and even if they did, they would have neglected it. They never experienced any kind of realization and never did any cultivation.

Here is a verse:

Ordinary people do not know that the mind is complete
If six supernatural powers are exercised freely such beings are unique
They do not use their mind for cultivation
Since they are not transformed into the buddha body, they remain as mortals

I was moved to tell these ecstasy addicts that the meaning of life was to spiritualize ourselves through cultivation. Otherwise, the soul would degrade and humankind would become degenerated. Wouldn't we be any different from animals that have no understanding of discipline?

The sage utters, "Food and sex are the nature of men!" This refers to human nature. People should not live only to indulge in food and sex. If this is the case, what separates us humans from animals? Hooked on the pills, these ecstasy addicts were simply a curious bunch bent on seeking a quick fix that was absolutely meaningless. They had simply squandered their lives away.

Only through enlightenment would the pure light of wisdom emerges, helping the individual surpasses the four forms of birth and the six realms of samsara and illuminating the path through the darkness of the three lower realms.

Ecstasy addiction corrodes the mind. It is just a complete waste of time. Evidently, all hard lessons experienced through drug addictions are self-inflicted. Have you found yourself? Who are you?

One of them said to me, "Who exactly are you? Are you a sage?"

I answered, "I'm not a sage. I'm only a hermit. A hermit who found himself."

"What did you find out about yourself?"

"I am Amitabha Buddha."

"You are Amitabha Buddha?"

Some of them were skeptical and others burst out laughing.

"Why don't you take refuge in Amitabha Buddha and go to the Western Pure Land!"

Someone incited the crowd and said, "Life is boring and worthless. Science and civilization bring about disasters. People have become more barbaric by engaging in killing, arson, and robbery. Society is full of violence. Only we, the ecstasy kids, understand emptiness and nothingness. We have found our comfort zone and so long as we are happy now, who cares about Amitabha Buddha, or pure light."

"True," the others agreed.

"Absolutely right. This is living in here and now!"

All of my reasoning was futile.

I shouted, "If you know that illusions are not real, then you must seek peace in the body and mind!"

"How do we seek peace in the body and mind?"

I recited a verse:

> **Within you there is Amitabha Buddha**
> **Who naturally exists as he is**
> **All you need to do is to seek him out within your heart**
> **Amitabha shall readily emerge**

One of the addicts heard this and left the circle of ecstasy addicts to follow me to chant the Buddha's name.

After a short journey, we met an angel of death [Grim Reaper].

He said to me, "I was about to chain them!"

I asked, "Where would you take them?"

The angel of death replied, "According to karmic retribution, these people loved to shake their heads and limbs, and they have become lost. They never thought about the future nor cared about the consequences on their actions. Therefore, they will be chained into the worm world."

"The worm world?" I was shocked.

The addict who followed me stuck his tongue out in astonishment after hearing this and felt no regrets following me. Life is truly meaningful when you discover your self-nature, engage your inner wisdom, give your best, go through the trials of tests, and practice diligently. Seeking sensual pleasure in life is just a waste of time and you will lose the direction of awakening to the "True Reality."

The angel of death replied, "According to karmic retribution, these people loved to shake their heads and limbs, and they have become lost. They never thought about the future nor cared about the consequences on their actions. Therefore, they will be chained into the worm world."

Sheng-yen Lu

22 Journey into the Home of a Disciple

While spiritual traveling, I heard someone chanting, "**OM GURU LIAN SHENG SIDDHI HUM**. Grand Master, help me! Grand Master, help me!" It was a distressful cry.

I stopped and entered the disciple's house. At first, I thought what the fuss was all about. Someone must be dying to make such an excruciating call.

This student must have heard my dharma talks because he burned the incense on two ends, which is used for emergency invocation. Originally, incense is burned on one end. However, he burned both ends and laid it flat on the incense burner to expedite a response.

As I entered his house, I was shocked not only to see him, his wife and their child but also thirty invisible ghosts that also lived in the house.

The house that he bought had very heavy negative energy. Not long after moving in, he set up his shrine and performed the boundary protection. The ghosts were the original occupants of this house and the boundary protection made them very uneasy. They were nonetheless powerful and could even enter the shrine.

The ghosts were also very rowdy. They made themselves appear in front of the child, and made him cry and become ill. He couldn't sleep during the day or night, and became a hyperactive child.

The couple also contracted strange illnesses. When they woke up in the morning, there were green and red spots on their skin. Furthermore, they dreamed that they were severely beaten by ghosts.

There were weird noises coming from the wall and things were moved. Pipes broke, the gas leaked for no reason, and the lights worked sometimes but failed other times. During the worst times, they even heard footsteps on the roof as though there were a group of twenty to thirty people marching. There were also gusts of foul odours in the house.

There were other disturbances.

One day when the couple was finishing their practice, they saw the statues on the shrine appear in a wrathful form with their tongues sticking out. They were laughing hysterically. This scared them and they cried out loud, claiming they were ghosts.

"We should write a letter to the True Buddha Quarter in Seattle, USA."

"But Guru has gone into retreat."

"The dakini will deliver the message to Guru, and he will do his practice to help us."

"I would definitely write a letter, but I will also light the incense on two ends."

"What exactly is lighting the incense on two ends?"

"Grand Master taught us to light the incense on two ends when there is an emergency."

I came to this student's house and saw these evil spirits. There were about thirty or so of them. In fact, it is normal for spirits to be present in a house.

Some houses have ancestral spirits, baby spirits, household spirits, earth deity spirits, visiting spirits, relative spirits, deity spirits, and earth bound spirits.

As long as there is peace and calm, and no one gets in the way of the other, and everybody minds their own business, it is considered normal.

The moment that I arrived at my student's house, the ghosts were taken aback and asked, "Who are you?"

I replied, "The Ghost King."

"The Ghost King? You certainly don't look like one," they were sceptical.

During the summer deliverance festival, I saw Guanyin Bodhisattva transformed into the "Scotch-Face Ghost King." So, I too turned into the "Scotch-Face Ghost King."

The Ghost King wears a hat that has Guanyin on top of it. His yellow beard hangs and waves in the air. His face is Scotch black, and he has wrathful eyes, exposed white teeth, and a long and bloody red tongue hanging out. In his right hand he carries a ghost-lock, and in his left hand he holds a ghost-hitting club.

The ghosts were scared by this sight and ran in all directions but they were repelled back by a "heaven and earth net." None of the ghosts could escape. They were very shocked and did not know what I was going to do with them. They were scared and trembled. They begged me, "We don't want to be reincarnated."

I said, "You guys have gone overboard."

They remained silent with their heads down.

I asked, "Is there anywhere else you guys can go?"

They replied, "We were living under the banyan tree. However, it was later cut down and a road was built on that spot. Because we had no place to live, we lived in this house. Now that Scotch-Face Ghost King is here, we don't know what to do next."

I asked, "Would you like to go to the West?"

Their eyes opened wide, "We teased the child, and made him cry and yell. We also teased the couple. It is lucky enough that we don't end up in hell, so why would the Scotch-Face Ghost King still want to take us to the Western Paradise? Are you sure you got the direction right?"

I said, "I will take all of you to Leaf Lake and teach you the Buddhadharma. Everybody can learn the Buddhadharma together and naturally, all of you will be reborn in the West."

Finally, they all nodded and followed me to Leaf Lake. At Leaf Lake, there were still many ghosts that were learning the Buddhadharma with me!

I taught them according to their individual natural capacity, starting from the easy practices to the difficult ones which included: absorption of mindfulness of the Buddha, Pratyutpanna samadhi, Hinayana meditation (emptying the ego), Mahayana meditation (emptying the ego and all things), ekagra or one pointed action [of body, speech and mind] samadhi, and absolute samadhi [the elimination of phenomena and the realization of the absolute].

I taught them how to chant the mantra, perform the homa, and enter samadhi.

Thus: "Returning the self to the origin as oneness. There are many expedient ways. The divine nature connects to all. Good or bad are means to the way."

I also taught them to develop good fortune and wisdom, and keep track of their practice. They started from the accumulation stage to the preliminary stage. From the preliminary stage to the stage of seeing the way, instantly reaching the first stage of bodhisattvahood, attaining the innate wisdom," and eventually one attains omniscience, which is realizing and validating the truth of all things.

Later one day, I was performing the "rice offering" and I visualized one bowl turning into another bowl, which then turned into many rows of bowls. Then I visualized that the land was filled with bowls and lastly, the entire space was filled with bowls of rice to feed all the ghosts.

As the ghosts ate the rice, one of them stood up and spoke to me, "Last year Grand Master wanted to take us to the Western Paradise, but we did not go. Now we have stayed at Leaf Lake for almost a year and have begun to realize that this place is only Leaf Lake, and not the Western Paradise!"

When I heard this, I kept quiet and did not say a word.

Another ghost stood up and said, "Now I understand it this way. All I have to do is to close and open my eyes, and I find myself in the Western Paradise of Ultimate Bliss. If I don't understand this, then I don't qualify to be Grand Master Living Buddha Lian-sheng, Sheng-yen Lu's student."

The third ghost stood up and said, "I finally understand that I have met Amitabha Buddha!"

The fourth ghost said, "When the Buddha taught the Dharma, he did so according to the natural capacity of each sentient being. There were some who gradually saw their Buddha-nature through a clear mind, while others were able to see it instantly. There are also Hinayana, Mahayana, Vajrayana, and teachings of non-existence and existence. Buddhism appeared in the divisions of primary stage of the Mahayana, the final stage of the Mahayana, the direct intuitive, teaching of perfection. There were also the Tripitaka doctrine, the interrelated doctrine, the shared doctrine and the perfect doctrine. All of these practices were very straightforward and understandable."

Then, at that moment, the sky was suffused with all hues of lights. The ghosts were amazed and delighted, and each of them could see lights of varying forms. Some saw rainbow lights, while others saw single-colored lights. Some saw pea-sized lights, while others saw lights in the form of sprinkles, a finger, and even the large dipper. There were also bright colorful clouds that rose up and down, which abruptly increased and shrunk in size.

Above the colorful clouds, a ghost king appeared. It was the "Scotch-Face Ghost King," who was the transformation of Guanyin Bodhisattva. Though he looked wrathful, he glowed and soothed the eyes of people. This was an inconceivable form manifested by the Tathagata out of his great compassion to reach sentient beings.

The Scotch-Face Ghost King said:

> There is no differentiation in space
> The immovable heavenly beings
> The pure wisdom ocean arises
> As firm as the Mount Meru
> Those supreme untainted beings
> The community of divine beings
> Surround Lian-sheng with great respect
> The vows of Living Buddha
> Shall never abandon a single being
> Swiftly fulfilling their wishes
> His merits and virtues are like the precious ocean
> As though Amitabha himself is present as the abbot

I put my palms together and so did the ghosts. The Scotch-Face Ghost King said:

"There is a region within the Western Paradise which is suited for both the ordinary people and sages. This region is further divided into two classifications, the first is called Community of Shared Defilement and the second is Community of Shared Purity. The Community of Shared Defilement is just like samsara, whose inhabitants include both ordinary people and sages. Living Buddha Lian-sheng does not lie. At Leaf Lake, there are also ordinary people and sages. These people constitute the Community of Shared Defilement. Today my appearance before you is attributed to the fact that you have all achieved either gradual or instant purification. Therefore, I will not forget my promise. I will take all of you to the Community of Shared Purity in the Western Paradise. Such merits are supremely wonderful, and unmatched by other merits."

All the ghosts rejoiced.

I put my palms together in respect and uttered, "Namo the thirty-six trillion, one hundred and nineteen thousand, and five hundred Amitabha Buddhas. I wish that sentient beings will always recite the name of the Buddha and be saved."

23 Feast with the Mountain King

I flew over a high mountain. It was not an ordinary mountain. Though it could not compare with mountains like Tai Shan, Heng Shan [in Hunan Province of China], Hua Shan, Heng Shan [in Shanxi Province of China], Song Shan and Kunlun Shan, it was well aligned with the "Directional Magnetic Energy."

Here's a verse:

> Tracking the dragon in the Zhen direction that aligns with the energy of the bagua
> The Zhen is mapped with the energy which sits in the east
> Within the fifteen degree to thirty degree of the Zhen direction
> One is blessed with fortune and prosperity of cattle and sheep
>
> In the Kan direction water energy may be disrupted, as one approaches the mountain
> Tracking the mountains and waters one understands the secrets of geomancy
> It is vital to know the energy points along the masculine Qian and feminine Kun

And understand how the seasons are set accordingly

In this mountain, the trees were green, the water meandered, the boulders and rocks shaped by nature appeared uniquely beautiful. Embraced by winds and clouds, the landscape resembled heavenly abode of the gods and immortals.

In fact you can observe movement and stillness in this mountain. The movement is water and cloud. The stillness is the trees and rocks. Yin and yang, movement and stillness; they are the very essence of spiritual practices. The immortals transform their nature and strengthen their bodies by cultivating qi to achieve unison with heaven and earth. They attain oneness this way.

It is described [by this verse]:

The Tao is within me
I am within the Tao
Neither within or outside
We all become one

As I traveled past the mountain, I remembered the days when I observed the stars and surveyed the land. This mountain was indeed an excellent mountain.

Suddenly, I saw many beings at the mountain top but they were not humans. By the appearance of their aura, I concluded they were not immortals nor malicious mountain or water spirits. They looked like they could be spirits that were nurtured by the earth's energy, and appeared godlike.

I waved my hands at them and they waved back.

One of them said, "Living Buddha Lian-sheng, Sheng-yen Lu, our mountain king wishes to invite you to our banquet."

"You recognize me?" I was surprised.

"You are the hermit of Leaf Lake. Who doesn't know you?!"

My initial reaction was the meeting may not seem right and the banquet may not turn out well, for it is said that one who is friendly may not approach you, but one approaches you may not be friendly.

(Though I had these thoughts it was not appropriate for me to tell them this.)

I asked, "Who is the mountain king?"

"You will know when you see him."

Without hesitation, I followed the group of people and entered an abode. The abode was made of jade that emitted serene lights. Right in the middle was a white-jade hall. Many palaces and towers abound. There was a platform that was decorated with the seven treasures and it had coral railings. There was a beautiful garden too. This dwelling was comparable to that of the most wealthy tycoon on earth would own.

There were seats that lined the main hall, which were all seated by spiritual beings. There was also a seat reserved for the mountain king and another one for me. I knew that this was definitely pre-arranged.

The mountain king was wearing a heavenly feathered garment when I saw him. I was astonished to recognize him as Chai, a fellow cultivator and friend of mine from earlier days. He once advocated that the human body had thirty-six thousand deities guarding every part of the body. Practitioners should regulate qi, increase saliva intake, in order to strengthen one's essence, qi, and spirit. One must also be pure in thought and meditate with single-mindedness.

Cultivator Cai also chanted the *Scripture of The Yellow Court* [*Huangting Jing*] and the Golden Light Mantra. He practiced by partaking the qi and swallowing saliva, and practiced purity and tranquility.

He liked:

To visualize the luminance of the three lights of the sun, moon, and stars

Connect to the heaven with closed eyes and a pure mind
Practice with one-thought
Thus becoming the mountain king

We were very happy to see each other, and he treated me to dinner and introduced me to everyone else. I knew some of them. Cai Mountain King was very sincere. Besides rare delicacies, the menu also included treasured dishes reserved for the immortals which were not normally served.

The following delicacies were specially prepared:
Beautifully-blossomed lotus
Calyx
Fine pearl powder
Ginseng as tasty as honey
Exotic herbs and flowers
Naturally formed celestial wine

I was overjoyed to eat these foods, even though they were impossible to obtain in the human world. I never thought that after such a long time of not seeing each other, our meeting would be this celebrative. I did not regret making the trip. This meeting was not coincidental, even if it was a one in a million chance occurrence.

There were plenty of drinks and food.

Cai Mountain King said, "Amitabha Buddha is different from lay people in terms of his enlightenment and non-delusion. However, the buddha mind and the mind of sentient beings are the same."

I replied, "The Western Pure Land may be billions of buddhalands away, it is only a hair's breath away for me. Intrinsically there is no difference between this shore and the other shore."

The mountain king said, "You said it well. There is no difference. You, Living Buddha Lian-sheng, Sheng-yen Lu must help me with a matter."

When I heard him, I was stunned.

"What kind of help?"

The mountain king replied, "There is one reason why I have invited you here. Residing on my mountain are so many mystic cultivators. Some specialize in the practices of "Primordial Origin of the Heaven," "Ancient Mirror," "Out of Body," "Inner View," "Origin of the Self," "Alchemy," "Flying Sword" and "Yin and Yang." The cultivators are really mixed. And in fact, several of them ascended to heaven and stole a rare celestial book, and some bottles of naturally formed celestial wine. They broke the heaven's rules. . ."

"Oh!" I was astonished.

No wonder the things I ate were not from earth nor were they from the Sumeru-based heavens. They were stolen from higher heavenly realm. I also consumed the celestial dishes, so didn't I break the heaven's rules too? What should I do now? I shouldn't have been so greedy and eaten all of the food.

The mountain king said, "I had to bring you here. Please forgive me. There are practitioners here who are good at divination. They specialize in lamp divination, the emperor yi-jing, wealth and longevity, weather prediction, astrological divination, among others. Based on their divination, they know that this mountain will be set ablaze by the divine fire."

"And what will happen when this mountain is set ablaze?"

"When the mountain is set ablaze, the practitioners will have nowhere to go. My cave will turn into a burnt wasteland, all plants on the mountain will turn into ashes, and everything will be wiped out."

"Why is it so serious?"

"It will be caused by the Fire Crow Battalion."

The mountain king and everyone else looked at me, and I was taken aback.

They put their palms together in a prayer's gesture and said, "We know that Living Buddha Lian-sheng, Sheng-yen Lu is a good friend of Zhu Rong the fire god. We want to ask you to discuss this with him."

I shook my head, "This is an infringement of the heavenly law. There is no negotiation!"

"Our lives are in your hand. Please reach out and help us!"

One of the practitioners even came and kneeled before me. Another one cried and recited a poem:

> **There is no solution to this case**
> **Breaking the heavenly law results in the burning of the mountain**
> **We beg you the compassionate Amitabha Buddha**
> **Please radiate your white lotus light**

I let out a sigh. I knew that although the mountain king and the other cultivators had not attained immortality, they were not evil spirits. Compassion arose from my heart and I nodded, biting my teeth. I was determined to help them no matter what.

Cai Mountain King and all practitioners cheered, "You do stand up for us!"

I advised, "Regardless of how long you live, how happy you are, and how many practices you have done, it is better to practice the right dharma, to go to the Pure Land, and be happy."

Everyone nodded in agreement.

The journey of intersecting the path of Zhu Rong the fire god and his Fire Crow Battalion took place.

I purposely asked the fire god, "Where are you going?"

Zhu Rong the fire god answered, "Off to set a mountain ablaze."

I asked, "How wide, how high, and how big is the mountain?"

He was instantly baffled by my question. As far as I know, Zhu Rong was the descendent Emperor Yan, the sun god, so as the water god "Gong Gong," the earth god, "Houtu," and the twelve-year cycle deity "Yeming." Emperor Yan had a daughter named "Yaoji," who was Lady Yunhua of Wu Mountain.

Lady Yunhua once told me, "At the extreme end of the southern hemisphere rules the Red Emperor Zhu Rong whose land stretches twelve thousand miles. Emperor Yan's wife gave birth to Yanju, Yanju had Jiebing, Jiebing had Xiqi and Xiqi had Zhu Rong. Zhu Rong was not good with numbers. He only knew how to set things on fire, regardless of what they were."

So I tested him and asked how wide, how high and how big the mountain was. Zhu Rong was dumbfounded.

I said, "Just burn that tree in the southern side of the mountain."

He asked, "How would this be setting the mountain on fire?"

I replied, "Didn't you know that a spark of fire can set the prairie ablaze. When a tree in the south of the mountain burns, it spreads from one tree to many trees. So won't the whole mountain get burned then?"

Zhu Rong laughed, "This is very true."

Zhu Rong led the Fire Crow Battalion and burned one tree in the southern side of the mountain. It was relaxing for all the other fire-crows, except for the one that had to do the burning. So the job was completed just like that.

I had earlier invited the "Water Emerald" God to station beside the tree. After the fire-crow had set the tree on fire and flew away, he would then spray water to put it out. If the fire was not put out, then it would certainly burn the whole mountain. Fire is fierce. At the adobe of the Golden Mother of the Jade Pond, it is surrounded by low buoyancy water and a ring of fire mountains. The mountains are bathed in a fire that cannot be put out even by the heaviest torrential rain. Therefore, the scenic landscape of the Jade Pond of the Golden Mother is almost impossible to reach!

I later heard that Cai Mountain King and all the practitioners were very grateful to me. Later, many of them cultivated the Amitabha Practice with faith, aspiration and practice, and were reborn in the Buddha Pure Land of the Western Paradise of Ultimate Bliss.

When the Heavenly Lord of Trayastrimsa Heaven learned about this incident, he reprimanded Zhu Rong. However, the Heavenly Lord was especially lenient towards Zhu Rong as they were distant relatives. Or perhaps it could be that he knew the character of Zhu Rong too well.

The Heavenly Lord knew about my involvement in this matter. He knew that the intention of my spiritual travel was to save people through the compassionate power of the Buddha, accepting all kinds of sentient beings without abandoning a single one of them, and benefit all regardless of whether they were good or bad. This is reaching out to sentient beings of all capacities, and accepting them as students regardless of their spiritual state.

This is the era of decline where the nature of man has degenerated. While I must deliver those who are involved with the spiritual path, even more so I must save the ordinary people who are bound to this earth.

I would like to write a verse about this incident:

> **You may say the Paradise of Ultimate Bliss is my home**
> **Laughing to myself, I travel spiritually across mountains and oceans**
> **Filled with compassion I stare at the setting sun**
> **Events in life are no different from the illusory sky flowers**

24 This is also Spiritual Travel

I once saw a person whose form of spiritual travel was somewhat inferior. Why was it inferior? First, he was flying very low. Second, his movement was not elegant and he couldn't control his movement. Third, he emitted a faint light.

I paid special attention to this person. Why? Because he wasn't behaving like a buddha or bodhisattva, an immortal, a godly being, a bardo spirit, or an elemental spirit. He was clearly still alive as a human being. How could he perform soul travel?

I had to follow him because I felt he was a dangerous person. He acted erratically like a drunk driver. Luckily, nothing bad happened. I followed him closely and finally, he found his way back to his place of residence. When I saw this place, I was taken aback. It was a psychiatric hospital.

So this traveller was a psychiatric patient. His soul had left his body in a dream and wandered around.

I laughed. He was as good as a homeless on the street.

I had initially wanted to leave the person alone but I discovered something strange about him. His body was emitting a faint light. I examined the light closer and discovered the light had come from an amulet. In fact, it was an amulet of True Buddha School. By relying on this light, he was able to avoid being possessed by evil spirits and demons. When I investigated further, I found out that his aunt was a disciple of True Buddha School.

When he was inflicted by illness, he began to sleepwalk. Later, he would go out of body while lying down. When he woke up, he would speak mainly in celestial lingo, claiming that he was the "Duke Wen," the "Red Boy," or the "Monkey King." In other instances, he claimed that he had stolen celestial peaches from the Golden Mother of the Jade Pond, or fought against twelve female angels and defeated them. He said that he was sent down by Living Buddha Ji Gong to help people on earth and also drank Ji Gong's celestial wine.

In short, he had many such stories.

Since he was wearing my amulet, I observed him for many days and discovered that his soul was in disarray. He was unsteady and hypersensitive. He saw many visions of illusions and deluded visions, and his karmic hindrances were heavy.

When he prayed to Duke Wen, he would mistake himself to be the emanation of Duke Wen patrolling the heavens in leisurely gaits.

When he entered the forest in his spiritual travel and monkeys attacked him, he would later claim that he was the "Red Child" who battled the Monkey King.

He also ate the dates from a garden, where he was surrounded by twelve butterflies. Thereafter, he would describe the incident as having stolen celestial peaches from the Golden Mother of the Jade Pond, where he fought and defeated twelve female angels who retreated and escaped. In fact, there were no angels in sight, just butterflies.

He drank dirty water from a cemetery and claimed that it was celestial wine. He was crazy yet he claimed that he was instructed by Living Buddha Ji Gong to descend upon earth to save people.

He ate a caterpillar and said that he defeated the White Lady.

This illustrates the behavioural pattern of this particular psychiatric patient.

What surprised me most was that he claimed he had been to the Western Paradise of Ultimate Bliss, where he had experienced delicately fine breeze blowing towards him, and heard chirping birds. He could eat or wear whatever he wanted. There was lots of freedom in this place. He could go anywhere. There were no worries and no need to work. Everything naturally grew from the land.

When I investigated further, I found out that he actually went to the Mulberry Kingdom. The mulberry trees there were huge. A light breeze was blowing and chirping birds were present. Silk worms ate the mulberry leaves that kept growing back. These silk worms discharged silk, which resembled heavenly garments that wrapped around like cocoons. The silk worms lived amongst the leaves and they were very carefree. They moved among the leaves which were so vast that they could never cover the whole area.

Due to the provision of the mulberry leaves, there was no need to work or worry about food, clothing, shelter, and moving around.

He treated the "Mulberry Kingdom" as if it were the Western Pure Land. I never would've imagined this.

It is written in *The Buddha Speaks of the Infinite Life Sutra of Adornment, Purity, Equality and Enlightenment of the Mahayana School*, Chapter 20 Virtuous Wind, Flower, and Rain:

> **At mealtimes in this buddha land, a natural breeze of virtue arises and gently blows over the nets and the various jeweled trees, resulting in exquisite sounds of the Dharma that expounds the doctrine of suffering, emptiness, impermanence, non-ego, and the respective paramitas, and along with these teachings, ten thousand kinds of delicate fragrances of virtue are diffused. If one smells those fragrances, one's impurities and habits spontaneously cease to arise. If touched by the breeze itself, one feels peace and comfort, and enjoys the same pleasure as a monk who has entered**

the Samadhi of Extinction.

Again, as the breeze blows amidst the seven treasure trees where flowers are scattered throughout the buddha land; they spontaneously divide into different colors, not mixed together. They are soft and pleasant to touch, glow brilliantly, and diffuse rich fragrances. When one's foot is placed on them, they sink down four inches, but when the foot is lifted, they rise to their former level. After mealtimes, the flowers vanish, leaving the ground clean without them. New rain follows and restores the whole place back to its original condition. At the right moment, six times a day, the breeze wafts, scattering the flowers in this way.

(It was this section of the sutra that made the patient mistake the Mulberry Kingdom to be the Western Pure Land.)

One must know the following points about the Western Paradise of Ultimate Bliss:

All sentient beings, whether they are born, in the process of being born, or are born immediately, are endowed with such fine bodies with majestic appearances. They will have immeasurable good fortune and virtues, clear wisdom, freedom, and possess supernatural powers. They will have enjoyments of all kinds in abundance, such as the palaces in which they dwell, their clothing, fragrant flowers, banners, and the various kinds of adornments. All of their wishes will come true.

Also there are lotuses of infinite colours of lights, and there is no name which describes time and age as it is infinite life. (It is definitely not Mulberry Kingdom.)

At first, I did not want to interfere with this psychiatric patient. This form of psychiatric illness tends to increase in the numbers, especially so in the cases of those who are possessed by evil spirits. When I saw that he was wearing the True Buddha School's amulet, however, I could not bear to see him like that. Let's just say that it was affinity because his amulet even had the picture of Padmakumara!

I stretched out my hand to grab his soul and sent it back to his body. Afterwards, I sealed the Baihui acupoint [crown chakra] on top of his head so that he could never leave his body and travel again.

Though he was young, he traveled too frequently and resulted in his health being fatigue and his mind remaining sleepy. His face appeared pale, so I invited the earth deity to watch over him and help him relax and sleep for two more days. When he woke up, he looked refreshed. He ate well and did not appear weak anymore.

The psychiatric doctor diagnosed him as a normal person again.

His family also discovered that he had suddenly recovered.

His aunt was the happiest person. She felt that the amulet was efficacious.

Only I knew that it was not a miracle that his illness was cured. His deliverance occurred due to our affinity. There are too many people in this world that need to be rescued. If I have to save all of them every time, there will be no end to the deliverance. All such cases of deliverance depend on affinity. When the affinity arises, I will deliver the person. Otherwise, I will just leave it for next time.

All sentient beings, whether they are born, in the process of being born, or are born immediately, are endowed with such fine bodies with majestic appearances. They will have immeasurable good fortune and virtues, clear wisdom, freedom, and possess supernatural powers.

Sheng-yen Lu

25 Sending a Relative to the Western Pure Land

I had a relative who believed in the practice of the Pure Land chanting of the Buddha's name since her youth. I always encouraged her to chant the Buddha's name at all times and told her not to stop chanting.

Let me briefly talk about the origin of the Pure Land School:

The Pure Land School was founded by the Venerable Master Huiyuan of Lu Shan or Lu Mountain and it is based on the three Pure Land Sutras, which are the *Contemplation Sutra of Amitayus*, the *Infinite Life Sutra*, and the *Amitabha Sutra*. In addition, there is also a treatise (sastra) known as *Treatise on Rebirth*. Master Huiyuan asserted that everyone should recite the Buddha's name and pray for rebirth in the Western Pure Land. Therefore, the name of the school was called the Pure Land School. Master Huiyuan was the first lineage master of the Pure Land School in China. Because Pure Land chanting is simple and easy to do, it is still very popular today. Most practitioners are very content to follow and practice it.

The Pure Land School is based on the principle that Amitabha Buddha had made forty-eight great vows and as long as one recites his name, one will be saved. Worldly beings have fallen into the sea of suffering and an endless cycle of reincarnation. They create karma and cannot save themselves. The Buddha, out of compassion, expounded the Pure Land Dharma so that people would become disenchanted by the world and seek ultimate bliss instead. As a result, they would make the vow to be reborn in the Pure Land. This was the finest and easiest teaching expounded by the Buddha.

Pure Land practice begins with "faith, aspiration, and practice." One must have faith or belief in the Pure Land, the aspiration to be reborn in the Pure Land, and practice according to the following four ways: chanting the Buddha's name, chanting with visualization, observing the Buddha's image while chanting, and mindfulness on the reality of the Buddha while contemplating on the Buddha. One can chant the Buddha's name while doing the Sixteen Visualizations [on the Pure Land] or one may chant without visualization. Due to the great vows and wholesome virtues of Amitabha Buddha, who accept beings in all karmic conditions to practice together, one must practice mindfully and at the time of one's death, one will be received by the Buddha.

Evidence for this teaching in the Pure Land School is found in the *Amitabha Buddha Sutra* which states: "If one's mind is wholeheartedly focussed on chanting the Buddha's name for seven days and seven nights, then at the time of death, one will be received by the Three Sages of the West and be reborn in the Pure Land as a lotus-born, and will enter into the stage of non-retrogression. In the Paradise of Ultimate Bliss, one can hear the Buddhadharma with joy and attain the realization of the patience acceptance of the awareness of the non-arising of all phenomena. All the accomplished people gather in one place and they can also travel in the ten directions to making offerings to the buddhas. They can also return to the Saha world to teach worldly beings."

Here is a verse:

> Believe in the Paradise of Ultimate Bliss in all of its majestic form
> Vow to be reborn in the West
> To leave suffering and attain happiness
> Practice the Buddhadharma
> And maintain a continuous stream of pure thoughts
> To attain spiritual fruition and meet Amitabha Buddha
> By listening to his Dharma one becomes enlightened

I once said, "In Vajrayana practice, one must also have the three provisions which are faith, aspiration, and practice. Once union is achieved in Guru Yoga and Personal Deity Yoga, never abandoning your guru and personal deity, you shall reach the Pure Land of your personal deity when you gain spiritual response.

Thus, in Vajrayana Buddhism there is the wisdom personal deity (external power), self-nature personal deity (own power), and all personal deities of the dharma realms (the dharma-realm power). Therefore, Vajrayana practice begins from the preliminary level to the advanced level. It is not suited for those with a low capacity because this practice aims to achieve buddhahood within this lifetime."

Now I wanted to talk about my relative who believed in the Pure Land chanting.

She was old and sick. (Old age and sickness are inseparable.)

At that time I was at Leaf Lake and I couldn't go to see her personally. However in my spiritual travel I knew that she was very ill. I also knew that she was connected to tubes and had undergone tracheostomy. It is described [by this verse]:

> Old age and illness can never end
> Don't be deluded any further, turn back immediately
> Illnesses are caused by karma
> Cleanse all karma and be liberated

When impermanence approached, I went to see my relative in my travel. I was shocked to see her ancestors, her husband, her eldest son, and all of her deceased relatives manifest in her consciousness. They were standing around her bedside, waiting to take her to the netherworld. We must remember that we should not follow any relatives that come to receive us at death. Due to our inability to sever our emotional ties with them, we will surely end up on the road to reincarnation.

Therefore, I immediately formed the Boundary Protection and set up the Adamantine Net to separate her from her ancestors, so that they couldn't get near her and take her away. Eventually they left and did not appear in front of her bed again. Because the Adamantine Net was there, I felt relieved.

I once gave her a set of my chanting beads. I whispered into her ears these words of advice:

"You must chant the Buddha's name! Just chant the Buddha's name!"

"If you can't verbalize the chanting, then chant inwardly with your heart."

"Wait until the Buddha comes to receive you before you go!"

She held tightly onto the chanting beads and recited "Namo Amitabha Buddha." Ever since she learned this chant in the "Buddha Chanting Hall" when she was young, she never forgot to chant. Though she never had much education in her life, she remembered to chant "Namo Amitabha Buddha," so this was indeed her good affinity.

I feel that it is not necessary in life to be honourable and rich. These things have to be earned through good merit acquired from past lifetimes. Some people enjoy high status while others have great wealth, living a blessed life of endless abundance. However, when I studied these things carefully, I realized that fame and fortune are not necessarily good spiritual affinity. They are just momentary illusions and temporary moments that vanish in an instant. The prime essence of one's life may not span a long time, hence the pursue of fame and fortune are never the right cause and intention for liberation.

One might as well learn from the example of this relative of mine. She had a difficult life and did not have much good fortune. However, she did learn the simple chant of "Namo Amitabha Buddha." As long as you focus singularly on chanting the Buddha's name until your mind is purified, then the purity of your heart shall reflect a pure inner land, and with this purity comes the lotus seat, and you will be reborn in a lotus flower. In the future, you shall meet the Buddha, attain realization of the unborn nature, and reside in the Buddha Land of Ultimate Bliss. This is more honourable and wealthier than those who have worldly fame and fortune.

How can worldly people know about the benefits of chanting the Buddha's name?

How can they know about the benefits of a purified mind?

How can they know that by chanting the Buddha's name until one-pointedness of mind is attained, one is released from all worries and afflictions?

There is a verse that goes like this:

The Western Paradise of Ultimate Bliss is regarded as supreme by many
We wish to advise all to enter this teaching
It is better not to spend time gossiping
But invest your time to chant the Buddha's name from dawn till dust

Though I commit to the practice of Vajrayana, I also advocate the chanting of the Buddha's name. In my Vajrayana practices, I revere Amitabha Buddha as my personal deity. I chant "Namo Amitabha Buddha" like the rest. I am the emanation of Padmakumara. Isn't the lotus kingdom the Paradise of Ultimate Bliss?

Here is a verse:

> **The great vows of the Western Paradise spread far and wide**
> **It is easiest to spread the teaching of chanting the Buddha's name**
> **Never cease to maintain a purified mind**
> **This pure practice is accepted by all schools**

While it is true that Vajrayana practice involves the purification of the body, speech, and mind, and teaches that through the empowerment of the personal deity, your self-nature personal deity shall emerge, you shall become realized and achieve buddhahood in your lifetime, your practice also requires you to continuously keep your thoughts pure!

On the day that my relative was about to pass away, it was amazing to note that she was totally aware of her departing. She saw the Three Sages of the West appear in space. Amitabha Buddha, Guanyin Bodhisattva, and Mahasthamaprapta Bodhisattva were present to receive her with the gift of a lotus seat. Seeing this, she was overjoyed and smiled.

She knew that she was about to depart, and she even kept pointing at the sky to tell everybody that the Three Sages of the West had appeared to receive her.

She bathed herself as a mark of purification. She held tightly onto the chanting beads I gave her. That very night, she left behind all suffering and gained rebirth to the Western Paradise of Ultimate Bliss in complete joy.

So what about myself? I continue to live in seclusion at Leaf Lake, and travel spiritually among the hills; sharing the crescent moon with the heavens, and in sweet slumber I shall rest on the mountain, watching the years rush by, and seeing how people go through the ups and downs of life. I can't help but sigh!

26 The Writing of Listening to the Inner Voice

Upon finishing my 166th book *Travel to Worlds Beyond*, I was overwhelmed with emotion, as there were yet many things I wanted to share. So, I contemplated writing another book about my innermost thoughts. This would be the 167th book entitled *Listening to the Inner Voice*. Its subtitle would be, *Enhance the Colors and Lustre of Your Dreams*.

I passed the days quietly at Leaf Lake. Everyday I gazed at the rays of sunshine at sunrise and watched the twilight of the sunset. Honestly speaking, I had my moments in life. I was showered with praise and glory. Those were the days where thousands of people welcomed me at the airport, thousands attended my ceremonies and thousands applauded me……

Presently I was living alone.

I never thought about what my future would hold. For example, would I return to Seattle from Leaf Lake? Or would I go back to Kaohsiung, the city of my childhood, or perhaps Taichung, the place where I entered adulthood? Would I spend my remaining days at Leaf Lake?

After completing *Travel to Worlds Beyond*, I practiced walking meditation in the mountain on a full moon night. Looking afar, I saw a sea of thin mist and suddenly, it seemed like my heart opened. I closed my eyes momentarily and quietly listened to the voice within.

These inner words contained both happiness and sadness. So, was it happiness or was it sadness? I did not even know. Either way, it felt like I had landed on the summit of the mountain, and was now watching the rolling clouds beneath me.

My life in Kaohsiung (my place of childhood), Taichung (where I grew up), Seattle (place of glory), and Leaf Lake (the place where I live in seclusion) flashed before me.

Should I be happy or sad?

Perhaps one day the Three Sages of the West, which are Amitabha Buddha, Guanyin Bodhisattva, and Mahasthamaprapta Bodhisattva, as well as other sages will build a dharma boat adorned with all kinds of treasure, whose light will shine everywhere. A necklace of precious stones will be placed over my neck and adorned my entire body with precious ornaments. Parasols with thousands of colours will be used to receive me, and wonderful and majestic heavenly beings will appear to reflect all of their splendour and lights. They shall receive my return to the Maha Twin Lotus Ponds, for I have attained the purification of the six roots, freed myself from all afflictions, abide in the stage of non-retrogression, and attain the fruition of buddhahood.

Perhaps I should ask myself, "Could I peacefully reach the other shore and forget all of my students without ever missing them?"

Wouldn't I be sad?

Wouldn't I be concerned?

What about the five million disciples of mine in samsara?

I felt that if I left the world, it would be inevitable that I would miss my students.

However, I would undoubtedly be sad if I stayed in this world too. So, both leaving and not leaving bring sadness. I always say, "Who would not have regrets?"

Perhaps I have scattered and left behind too many fragments of my sentiments in this world, so much so that it would be impossible to clean them up. For this reason I felt my heart was burdened with such emotion. Even the lustrous dharma boat could not carry me away.

Let me pen a poem about *Listening to the Inner Voice*:

> **No one can live forever**
> **Growing old in the human world**
> **The dharma boat approaches**
> **I no longer can hold back my tears**
>
> **Such sentimental burden weighs on me**
> **The words I have said**
> **Are said over and over again**
> **Sadness suddenly overcomes me**
> **Turning me into a naked child**
>
> **There will come a day**
> **The day of the last page**
> **The last page of my writing**
> **All of you can contemplate this**
> **Please listen to my vows**
> **I am willing to bring all of you**
> **Everyone of you**
> **Away from here**

Living Buddha Lian-sheng, Sheng-yen Lu

Sheng-yen Lu
17102 NE 40th CT.
Redmond, WA 98052
U.S.A.

Perhaps I have scattered and left behind too many fragments of my sentiments in this world, so much so that it would be impossible to clean them up. For this reason I felt my heart was burdened with such emotion. Even the lustrous dharma boat could not carry me away.

Sheng-yen Lu

Significance of Taking Refuge

Taking refuge means to accept guidance, reliance and deliverance.

The heart of taking refuge lies in one word: faith. Faith is the beginning of all endeavors, just as the saying goes:

> **Faith is the basis of the path, the mother of virtues;**
> **Nourishing and growing all good ways,**
> **Cutting away the net of doubts,**
> **Revealing the unsurpassed road to enlightenment.**

The doctrine of faith, understanding, practice, and realization as taught in Buddhism begins with faith.

Taking refuge and receiving the respective empowerments are similar to a student officially registering for enrollment in school. When one receives the empowerment from Living Buddha Lian-sheng and takes refuge in him, one also receives the lineage transmission of True Buddha School and formally becomes a disciple of the school. One's negative karma gradually dissolves, and one is protected by the thirty-six benevolent deities. One also receives all kinds of merits, and does not easily fall into the Three Evil Paths. Therefore, one is able to swiftly accumulate good karma, and eventually realize supreme enlightenment.

From the discussion above, one can thus see that the ritual of taking refuge and empowerment is a holy and noble undertaking. Once one receives the refuge empowerment, one truly enters the gate of practicing Buddhism and becomes a True Buddha disciple.

However, taking refuge is not the same as ordination (becoming a monk or nun). Any ordination must have the written and signed consent from one's parents or spouse, and it must be officially approved by the highest authority of True Buddha School.

The Sutrayana tradition practices the Threefold Refuge, whereas the Vajrayana tradition practices the Fourfold Refuge.

In the Fourfold Refuge, the meaning of the Sanskrit word "Namo" is to take refuge.

> **Namo Guru bei – I take refuge in the Root Guru.**
> **Namo Buddha ye – I take refuge in the Buddha.**
> **Namo Dharma ye – I take refuge in the Dharma.**
> **Namo Sangha ye – I take refuge in the Sangha or the ordained.**

Significance of Taking Refuge in Living Buddha Lian-Sheng and True Buddha School

The Merits of Taking Refuge

Living Buddha Lian-sheng has the dharma title of "Great Blessing Vajra" and he is the Root Guru of True Buddha School. True Buddha disciples who cultivate the Root Guru Practice will be able to achieve spiritual union and responses from the Root Guru, which is a great blessing. With the Root Guru's blessing, one can gain health, long life, a harmonious family, fortune, wisdom, and the fulfillment of all wishes in the mundane realm. In the transcendental realm, one attains bodhisattvahood.

According to the *Sutra of Consecration,* students are protected by thirty-six guardians after taking refuge, which are sent by the Four Heavenly Kings (devarajas). If these students can also cultivate the Root Guru Practice, then Vajrayaksa, his retinue of five hundred, and multitudes of bodhisattvas will also provide protection.

All students who take refuge and receive the necessary empowerments shall, through the diligent cultivation of the Root Guru Practice, benefit both themselves and others due to the boundless merits of the Root Guru Practice. All transgressions will be extinguished and all evil shall depart. The Root Guru Practice is the most efficacious of all practices and should be widely propagated.

The Methods of Taking Refuge

At 7:00 a.m. (your local time), on either the first or the fifteenth of every lunar month, face the direction of the rising sun. With palms joined, reverently recite the Fourfold Refuge Mantra three times: "Namo Guru bei, Namo Buddha ye, Namo Dharma ye, Namo Sangha ye. Seeking Living Buddha Lian-sheng's guidance, I am taking refuge in the True Buddha," and prostrate three times.

Send a letter to the True Buddha Foundation to indicate your wish to receive the refuge empowerment. State your name, address, age, and enclose a voluntary offering to the contact address of Living Buddha Lian-sheng. Upon receiving the letter, the True Buddha Foundation will process your request. The address is:

Grand Master Sheng-yen Lu
17102 NE 40th Ct.
Redmond, WA 98052
U.S.A.
Tel: 425-885-7573
Fax: 425-883-2173

Upon receiving the refuge request letter, the True Buddha Foundation will send you a refuge certificate, a picture of Living Buddha Lian-sheng, and instructions on how to start cultivation of the Four Preliminary Practices.

You may obtain refuge empowerment personally from Grand Master Lu, or from a True Buddha acharya who confers the empowerment on behalf of Grand Master, by visiting a True Buddha temple, chapter, cultivation group, or by attending a True Buddha ceremony.

Taking refuge and receiving the respective empowerments are similar to a student officially registering for enrollment in school. When one receives the empowerment from Living Buddha Lian-sheng and takes refuge in him, one also receives the lineage transmission of True Buddha School and formally becomes a disciple of the school.

Glossary

-A-

Abhidharma School
Buddhist school based on the sastras, which are the doctrinal commentaries, philosophical works, discourses, discussions, treatises on the dogma, and doctrines of Buddhism which summarize key points and classify teachings.

Acharya (Sanskrit, literally "Teacher")
A supreme teacher within Vajrayana Buddhism. The acharya may conduct ceremonies or bestow teachings and empowerments according to the acharya's level. Synonymous with "vajra master."

Agama Sutras
The four sections of the buddhist canon recorded by five hundred of Shakyamuni Buddha's disciples during the First Council which took place immediately after the Buddha's Parinirvana. The four sutras are: *The Dirgha Agama*, *The Madhyama Agama*, *The Samyukta Agama* and *The Ekottara Agama*.

Amitabha (Sanskrit, literally "Boundless Light")
As one of the Five Dhyani Buddhas, he is the chief buddha of the Lotus Family and he is typically depicted with a red body and holding the Meditation Mudra.

Arhat (Sanskrit, literally "Worthy One")
One who has conquered the emotions and ignorance that keep one locked in samsara, achieved the goal of the Theravada (Hinayana)

tradition, experienced the cessation of suffering, and attained the state of liberation.

Avalokitesvara Bodhisattva (Chinese - Guanyin, literally "She Who Observes the Sounds of the World")
She is the bodhisattva of compassion. She has various forms including the two armed, four armed, or the thousand armed and thousand eyed Avalokitesvara. Guanyin is one of the most important bodhisattvas in Buddhism and is a principal deity in True Buddha School. Guanyin is usually depicted as female in China and Japan, and as male in other parts of Asia.

Avatamsaka Sutra (The Flower Garland Sutra)
This sutra was preached by the Buddha after his enlightenment. The purpose of this sutra is to explain world as it appears to an enlightened buddha or bodhisattva, with detailed description of the course of the bodhisattva practice.

Avici Hell
The eighth and most painful of the eight buddhist hells. It is the lowest level of the hells, in which suffering is the greatest and longest.

-B-

Bagua (Chinese, literally "Eight Diagrams")
Also known as "trigrams", these eight diagrams are: (1) heaven (qian); (2) earth (kun); (3) thunder (zhen); (4) wind (xun); (5) lake (dui); (6) water (kan); (7) fire (li); (8) mountain (gen). In Taoist cosmology, they represent reality.

Bardo Body
This is the formless body, or soul, which is in the state between death and rebirth.

Bhiksu
A male practitioner who has renounced worldly life and taken the pledge to observe the 250 precepts of a fully ordained monk in order to attain liberation from samsara.

Bhiksuni
A female practitioner who has renounced worldly life and taken the pledge to observe the 500 precepts of a fully ordained nun in order to attain liberation from samsara.

Bodhi (Enlightenment)
The goal of all buddhists. Only through enlightenment can we overcome samsara and enter nirvana.

Bodhicitta (Sanskrit, literally "Awakened Mind")
The key to Mahayana Buddhism, it refers both to an enlightened mind and to the resolution arising for the profound compassion to attain an enlightened mind for the purpose of assisting all beings.

Bodhidharma
The First Patriarch of Zen Buddhism. He came from Southern India to China during the Liang Dynasty. His method emphasized the importance of serene meditation and inward contemplation, expressing the Buddha-mind and focusing on the practice of concentration and purification.

Bodhisattva (Sanskrit, literally "Wisdom Being")

One who has developed the altruistic motive of attaining enlightenment to help all sentient beings. There are ten stages in the process of becoming a bodhisattva.

Buddha
An enlightened being who has perfected compassion and wisdom, and has realized the dharmakaya, sambhogakaya and nirmanakaya.

Buddhadharma
The teachings of Buddhism.

Buddhahood
The stage of enlightenment.

-C-

Chan Sect (Zen Sect)
A Mahayana buddhist School that originated by Bodhidharma in China that later took root in Japan. It emphasizes the practice of sitting in meditative absorption and de-emphasizes rituals and intellectual studies.

Cien School (Dharmalaksana School, Faxiang School)
Also known as Yogacara. It is based on the *Lankavatara Sutra,* the *Samdhinirmocana Sutra,* the *Vijnaptimatratasiddhi Sastra* and the *Yogacarabhumi Sastra.*

City God (Cheng Huang)
A common Taoist deity who controls the spirits within a certain area (a town or city).

Consecration (Eye Opening Ceremony)

After a buddhist altar is set up, a practitioner may have a vajra master or reverend perform this ceremony so that the respective deities on the altar descend and thus become "alive."

-D-

Dakini
A female wisdom being or protector of tantric practitioners.

Devakaya (Sanskrit, literally "Goddess")
A celestial maiden or female deity.

Dharani
Originally, it could be a seed syllable, a mantra, a sutra, or sastra. A practitioner would recite it to help increase memory, increase wisdom, decipher right from wrong, allow one to not be angered, and would teach one the forty-two root seed syllable sounds. In modern times, it is generally referring to a long mantra.

Dharma
The body of teachings expounded by Shakyamuni Buddha. It is roughly equivalent to phenomenon, a basic unit of existence and/or experience.

Dharmakaya
See Trikaya.

Diamond Sutra
An important teaching of Shakyamuni Buddha in which he shows that all things are ultimately empty and devoid of any inherent reality, including the idea of self, others, and dharma.

-E-

Earth Deity
A deity who protects the area around a house or temple. He is said to be a god of wealth and merit.

Eight Sufferings
These are: suffering of birth, suffering of old age, suffering of sickness, suffering of death, suffering of being apart from the loved ones, suffering being together with the despised ones, suffering of not getting what one wants, and suffering of the flourishing of the five skandhas.

Eightfold Path
Categorized under the following headings: right understanding, right thought, right speech, right action, right livelihood, right effort, right mindfulness, and right contemplation.

-F-

Fire Puja
See Homa.

Four Deva Kings
There are Four Heavenly Kings who dwell on Mount Meru, guard the four gates at the four compass points of Indra's Heaven, and are considered guardians of Buddhism. Dhrtarastra guards the east, is white colored, holds a stringed instrument, and is the king of the Gandharvas (celestial musicians). Virudhuka guards the south, is blue colored, holds a sword and is the king of the Khumbanda (giant demons). Virupaksa guards the west, is red colored, holds a serpent and a jewel, and is the king of the Serpent Gods. Vaisravana guards the north, is yellow colored and holds a banner in his right hand

and a mongoose in this left hand, and is the king of the Yaksas (wild demonic beings) - he is also called the Yellow Jambhala.

-G-
Garuda
Great golden-winged birds. They are considered to be half animal and half god. They used to eat dragons from the ocean until the Dragon King pleaded to the Buddha to have him help convince the garudas to stop eating the dragons. The Buddha agreed to have all reverends make daily offerings to the garudas in exchange for not eating anymore dragons. They serve as protectors and helpers to dharma practitioners.

Golden Mother of the Jade Pond
A powerful Taoist deity; associated with the peach of immortality, she bestows longevity to beings; she helped Living Buddha Lian-sheng begin his spiritual practice and therefore is usually one of the primary deities on True Buddha School temple altars.

Guanyin Bodhisattva
See Avalokitesvara.

Guru Yoga
In Vajrayana Buddhism, the guru is the embodiment of the Triple Jewels - the Buddha, Dharma and Sangha. To practice the Guru Yoga is to merge with the mind-stream of one's guru, thus becoming one with the Triple Jewels and all the lineage gurus. True Buddha School's Guru Yoga is a standardized procedure which includes reciting mantras, forming mudras, and doing visualizations.

-H-

Hariti
As told in the *Lotus Sutra*, she was a cannibalistic demon who had hundreds of children, but abducted, killed, and ate the children of others. The bereaved mothers of her victims went to Shakyamuni Buddha to ask him to put a stop to her murders. The Buddha stole Hariti's youngest child and hid him under a begging bowl. She went to the Buddha for help and he made her understand how it felt to have one's child missing and asked if she could imagine the suffering of parents whose children had been devoured. Shakyamuni told her that from then on all reverends would make offerings to her on a daily basis to satisfy her hunger and thirst so that she would not eat the children of others.

Hinayana
A term used by the later Mahayana School to describe the original school of Buddhism. Since the Hinayana School focused on liberation for oneself, the Mahayana School deemed it the "Lesser Vehicle," as it did not work for the liberation of all beings. Presently, the Hinayana School refers to itself as Theravada (School of the Elders) which is the only surviving sect of Hinayana and is based mainly in Southeast Asia. The Hinayana School emphasizes that the way to attain liberation is through one's own meditation and through living a monastic lifestyle.

Homa (Fire Puja, Fire Offering)
A fire ritual used as a means of offering to buddhas, bodhisattvas, dharma protectors or spiritual beings. They are performed in order to increase merit, eradicate negative karma, increase wealth, and increase harmony and good health.

-I-

-J-

Ji Gong (Daoji)
Typically depicted as a smiling monk, wearing tattered monastic robes, and carrying a bottle of wine and a magical fan. He was awarded the title of "Living Buddha Ji Gong" because he defended people against injustice, rewarded virtue, and helped the poor. He was expelled from the monastery where he resided due to his eccentric behavior which broke the rules of the Vinaya (e.g., he ate meat and drank wine).

-K-

Kalpa
An eon, widely used in ancient India to measure time. Kalpas are uncountable; there is no precise number of years involved. A kalpa can be referred to the four stages of the rise and fall of a universe: rise, continue, decline, and chaos.

Kamadhatu Realm (Desire Realm)
The realm of sensuous desire. The beings in this realm are dominated by the desires of sex and food. This realm includes the six heavens of desire, the human realm, the animal realm and the hells.

Karma (Sanskrit, literally "Action" or "Deed")
The cycle of cause and effect; concept believed amongst the buddhist, Hindu, Jain and Sikh traditions.

Ksitigarbha Bodhisattva (Sanskrit, literally "Womb of the Earth")
Ksitigarbha has a vow to not reach buddhahood until all the hells are empty.

Kurukulla Buddha Mother
The deity of magnetism and harmony. She has a red body and holds a flowery bow and arrow for love and desire.

-L-

Lord Yama (Yama King, Yama, Deva, Hell King, Lord Yama)
The Lord of Death. He is known as the king of the netherworld and the head of karmic punishment of those who reside in hell.

-M-

Maha Twin Lotus Ponds
This is the Pure Land of the Padmakumara located in the Western Paradise of Amitabha Buddha. By practicing the True Buddha Tantra, one may travel to the Maha Twin Lotus Ponds in meditation or at the time of death.

Mahasattva
One who reaches the tenth stage of Bodhisattvahood and decides to forgo complete enlightenment in order to help others.

Mahasthamaprapta Bodhisattva (Sanskrit, literally "Of Great Power")
A companion of Amitabha Buddha in both Chinese and Japanese Buddhism who represents the wisdom of Amitabha Buddha. With Avalokitesvara Bodhisattva on the left of Amitabha Buddha, and Mahasthamaprapta on the right, they are called the "Three Holy Ones of the Western Paradise."

Mahayana Buddhism (Sanskrit, literally "Great Vehicle")
The latter of the two major schools of Buddhism which emphasizes liberating all sentient beings from suffering. It is practiced by the

schools of Pure Land, Zen, and Vajrayana Buddhism.

Manjushri Bodhisattva (Sanskrit, literally "He who is noble and gentle")
The Bodhisattva of Transcendent Wisdom. He is typically depicted with the *Prajnaparamita Sutra* and a sword which cuts through the clouds of ignorance.

Mara
Demons or demonic influences which are essentially the same as what is more commonly known as "devil." They manifest in the form of greed, anger, ignorance, jealousy, and other emotions.

-N-

Naga
A serpent-like spiritual being living in caves, rivers and heavens who often guards great treasure. They are considered to be half animal and half god.

Nagarjuna (second century AD)
Born into a Brahmin family in southern India. He could commit any sutra to memory. After renunciation he completed reading Tripitaka (the three buddhist canons) in ninety days and gained penetration into all profound doctrines. Since his ancestral link could be traced to the nagas or dragons of northern India, he was able to enter the dragon palace under the ocean and study all the Mahayana scriptures that were being kept there, make records, and bring the scriptures back. This was the reason why Mahayana Buddhism flourished. He was taught by Vajrasattva and from these teachings he wrote *The Madhyamika Sastra*, which later became the most important sas-

tra for the Three Sastra School. Since he received the lineage from Vajrasattva, the official establishment of Vajrayana named him as its founder.

Naropa (1016-1100)
A scholar at the famous Nalanda University who left to follow the noted yogi, Tilopa. He is known for the Six Yogas of Naropa which form a major part of the practices of the Tibetan Kagyu School.

Nirmanakaya
See Trikaya.

Nirvana (Sanskrit, literally "Cessation")
Cessation of suffering where one is freed from the cycle of rebirth. It is a state where one realizes one's connection with the absolute.

-O-

OM GURU LIAN SHENG SIDDHI HUM
The Heart Mantra of Padmakumara (Living Buddha Lian-sheng).

-P-

Padmakumara (Sanskrit, literally "Lotus Youth")
The sambhogakaya (bliss body) of Living Buddha Lian-sheng. He is a great fortune-bestowing and hindrance removing bodhisattva. For more details about Padmakumara and his abode, the Maha Twin Lotus Ponds in the Western Paradise, see the *True Buddha Sutra*.

Padmasambhava (Sanskrit, literally "Lotus Born")
Commonly known as the Second Buddha, after Shakyamuni Bud-

dha, he was supremely accomplished in the esoteric arts, used his powers to defeat many demons and black magic (Bon) practitioners in Tibet in the eighth century and founded the Nyingma tradition of Tibetan Buddhism. He is one of the principal deities of True Buddha School.

Paradise of Ultimate Bliss
See Western Paradise.

Paramitas
See Six Paramitas.

Personal Deity (Yidam)
One of the Three Roots (Guru, Yidam and Dharma Protector) of Vajrayana practicioners. One begins to practice the Yidam Yoga after attaining spiritual responses in the Fourfold Preliminary Practices and the Guru Yoga. A practitioner chooses one of the eight major deities of True Buddha School (Padmakumara, Amitabha Buddha, Avalokitesvara Bodhisattva, Ksitigarbha Bodhisattva, Maha Cundi Bodhisattva, Yellow Jambhala, Padmasambhava, or Medicine Buddha) and practices the personal deity yoga throughout one's lifetime.

Prajna
The most profound wisdom. It is not the same as knowledge or intelligence, but a more subtle and deeper level of wisdom.

Pratyeka-buddha (Solitary Realizer)
A practitioner who attains nirvana without a human teacher, but does not go on to teach others the path towards enlightenment.

Pure Land
A realm of consciousness founded by a buddha. By being reborn in

-Q-
Qi
Energy which can leak from the mind via craving, greed, anger, ignorance, and wrong views. To cultivate the mind is to cultivate qi, and to cultivate qi is to cultivate the mind.

-R-

Ragaraja
Appear with two heads, as well as the form with a single head, has three eyes, sits on a lotus throne, and has six arms where each arm carries a ritual implement, the most significant being the bow and arrow. When he shoots at the hearts of sentient beings, he brings them love and passion.

Raksasa
Evil and violent demons referred to as "man-eaters."

Raksasi
A female Raksasa.

Relic (Sariras)
When a practitioner dies and is cremated, small pearl and jewel like objects are found in the remaining ashes which may multiply or radiate light.

Rinpoche (Tibetan, literally "Precious One")
A title reserved for incarnate lamas and accomplished teachers.

(a pure land, the aspirant can continue spiritual development without fear of retrogression.)

-S-

Samadhi (Sanskrit, literally "Make Firm")
The state of consciousness where the meditator becomes one with the object of meditation, and there is no separation between the meditator and the object of meditation. It is a non-dualistic state.

Samantabhadra Bodhisattva (Sanskrit, literally "Universal Kindness")
The Primordial Buddha who originated the teaching of the Dzogchen (Great Perfection). He is the Primordial Buddha of the Nyingma School and an emanation of Vairocana. He is typically depicted holding the wish-fulfilling jewel in his left hand and holding his right hand in the teaching mudra (the index and thumb touch while the other three fingers extend upward). His limitless compassion miraculously appears in all buddha pure lands, and his teachings are given without the use of language.

Sambhogakaya
See Trikaya.

Samsara (Sanskrit, literally "Running Around")
Comprised of the six realms: devas (gods), asuras (jealous gods), humans, animals, hungry ghosts, and beings in hell. Sentient beings are stuck in the six realms until they attain enlightenment and realize that the realms are merely states of consciousness, thus freeing them of the need to be reborn in one of these realms.

Sangha
A Sanskrit word meaning "community," "assembly," or "association with a common goal." In Buddhism, it refers to monks or nuns with a higher realization, though in modern times this term has been

used to describe groups of buddhist followers in general. It is responsible for teaching, spreading, translating, and maintaining the teachings of the Buddha.

Sangharama (Guanyu)
A dharma protector and guardian of temples. In temples, he is always paired with Skanda (Wei Tuo), with Sangharama on the left and Skanda on the right (when facing the shrine).

Sariputra
Originally known as Upatisya, he was the son of a Brahman scholar. Before taking refuge in the Buddha, he had already acquired many students of his own, and he eventually led three hundred and fifty students to take refuge in the Buddha. He was renowned for his great wisdom, was the principal disciple of Shakyamuni Buddha, and the person most trusted by the Buddha. He followed the Buddha for more than forty years, during which not one single thought of displeasure or dissatisfaction with the Buddha arose in him. He entered into the tranquil realm of nirvana before the Buddha did.

Satkayadrsti
The false belief in a permanent individuality.

Satyasiddhi Sect
One of the ten major schools of Chinese Buddhism. It is based on *The Satyasiddhi Sastra* written during the fourth century by Harivarman, a buddhist monk from central India.

Shakyamuni Buddha
Siddhartha Gautama was born in Lumbini, India (modern day Nepal) sometime between 563 BCE and 483 BCE. He later became known as Shakyamuni Buddha. "Shakya" was his clan name and

"muni" means great sage, thus, "the great sage of the Shakya clan." At the age of twenty-nine he left his home, and achieved enlightenment under the Bodhi Tree at age thirty-five. He became the founder of Buddhism and spread the dharma to all beings.

Six Paramitas (Six Perfections of the Bodhisattva Way)
These are: generosity, discipline, patience, diligence, meditation, and wisdom.

Six Realms of Reincarnation
See Samsara.

Six Supernatural Powers
These are: divine vision (instantaneous view of anything, anywhere, in the form realm), divine hearing (perception of human and divine voices), perception of the thoughts of other beings, mindfulness of previous existences, divine speed (power to be anywhere at will), and knowledge concerning the extinction of one's own impurities and passions (which signifies with certainty of having attained liberation).

Sixth Patriarch (Huineng - 638 AD - 713 AD)
A Chinese Zen master who is one of the most important figures in the entire tradition. He was the last lineage master to receive the dharma robe.

Skanda (Wei Tuo)
A guardian devoted to protecting buddhist temples and practitioners. In temples, he is always paired with Sangharama (Guanyu), with Skanda on the right and Sangharama on the left (when facing the shrine).

Skeleton Visualization Method
Meditation technique taught by Shakyamuni Buddha. It involves visualizing self turning into bones and is used as an aid to help one realize the emptiness of the ego.

Sravaka (Sound-hearer)
One who attains enlightenment by being a disciple of, and hearing the teachings of a living buddha.

-T-

Tao (Dao)
Means "the path to the truth."

Tathagata (Sanskrit, literally "Thus Come One")
A synonym for Buddha. It refers to the primordially pure Buddha-nature which can neither be created anew nor ever destroyed. This nature can remain obscured indefinitely if not purified and developed.

Tathagatagarbha
See Tathagata.

Ten Paramitas
These are: generosity, discipline, patience, diligence, meditation, wisdom, expedient means, vow, power, and omniscience.

Three Sastra School (Madhyamika School)
School based on three sastras translated by Kumarajiva: *The Madhyamika Sastra* (*The Treatise of the Middle Way*), *The Dvadashamukha Sastra* (*The Twelve Aspects Treatise*), and *The Shatika Sastra* (*The Twelve Aspects Treatise*). The primary sastra, *The Madhyamika Sastra*,

was written by Nagarjuna and is described as a system of sophistic nihilism, dissolving every proposition into a thesis and its antithesis, and then refuting both.

Tiantai School (Heavenly Terrace Mountain Sect)
It is one of the ten major schools of Chinese Buddhism primarily based on the *Lotus Sutra*. Master Zhiyi (531-597 AD) established this Mahayana school on the Tian Tai Mountain during the Sui Dynasty. He taught the rapid attainment of buddhahood through the practice of observing the mind and emphasized both scriptural study and practice.

Trayastrimsa Heaven
A heavenly realm above the realm of the Four Heavenly Kings, on top of Mount Meru. According to tradition the Buddha spent time there teaching the Abhidharma to his mother, who was reincarnated into this realm. There are thirty-three heavens within this realm and all are governed by Indra.

Trikaya (Sanskrit, literally "Three Bodies")
The three bodies referred to are the nirmanakaya (emanation body), sambhogakaya (bliss body), and dharmakaya (dharma body), all of which are manifestations of the Buddha. For example, Living Buddha Lian-sheng is the nirmanakaya - a physical form of the Buddha in the Saha world. Padmakumara is the sambhogakaya - a subtle form of the Buddha which usually appears to humans in meditation, visions and dreams. The dharmakaya of Living Buddha Lian-sheng is a manifestation of the Buddha that is timeless, formless and is one with the universe.

Tripitaka
The three parts of the Pali canon, consisting of: the Sutras (the teach-

ings given by the Buddha), Vinaya (the rules of monastic life), and the Sastras (Abhidharma).

Triple Jewels (Triple Gems)
The three precious entities of Buddhism in which all buddhists take refuge in; they are the Buddha, Dharma, and Sangha.

True Buddha
The word "true" in this context is not used to compare true and false, thus creating a duality and contradicting all that Buddhism actually professes. The dharma of True Buddha School is true because it helps practitioners calm their minds and let go of ignorance, hatred and greed. The pure land of True Buddha School, the Maha Twin Lotus Ponds, is true because people have been there and seen it. The sequence of practices (outer practices, inner practices, secret practices and most secret practices) are true because one will gain the appropriate spiritual responses while following this sequence. Living Buddha Lian-sheng is the True Buddha because all sentient beings are the True Buddha.

True Buddha Quarter
The True Buddha Quarter serves as the headquarters for the True Buddha Foundation, the core governing body of True Buddha School.

True Buddha School
In 1975, Living Buddha Lian-sheng established Ling Xian Zong in Taiwan and he officially changed its name to True Buddha School on March 1, 1983. In 1985 Living Buddha Lian-sheng established the main True Buddha School temple, the Ling Shen Ching Tze Temple in Seattle, which was dedicated to the propagation of the True Buddha Tantra.

Twelve Divisions of the Mahayana Canon
The Mahayana buddhist Canon consists of the Tripitaka, dharma analysis, and many sutras that are not contained in Hinayana Buddhism. The canon is organized into twelve major topics.

-U-

-V-

Vairocana Buddha
Also known as the Great Sun Buddha, he is one of the Five Dhyani Buddhas. He is typically depicted as white in color and holds either the Dharmachakra Mudra or the Supreme Wisdom Mudra.

Vaisravana
See Four Deva Kings.

Vajra (Sanskrit, literally "Diamond Scepter")
A common ritual object in Vajrayana buddhist practices which represents a thunderbolt, or diamond, which in turn represents being indestructible. It can symbolize the male aspect of enlightenment (skillful means), whereas the vajra bell represents the feminine aspect of enlightenment (wisdom).

Vajra Protector (Dharma Protector, Wrathful Protector)
Enlightened beings that take on wrathful forms. Their function is to protect buddhist practitioners.

Vajrayana
A major branch of Buddhism in which the guru teaches an accelerated path to enlightenment, using the techniques of chanting mantras, forming mudras and visualization.

Vasumitra
It was written in the *Avatamsaka Sutra* that the monk Sudhana sought advice from over fifty beings during his pilgrimage, one of them was a courtesan known as Vasumitra Bodhisattva.

Vidyadhara
One who has attained mastery in the tantric practices and is endowed with various magical powers.

Vinaya School
Founded by Master Daoxuan (596-667 AD) during the Tang Dynasty in China. It focuses on one of the three parts of the Tripitaka which emphasizes on precepts, discipline, vows, conduct, and ethics.

-W-

Western Paradise (Western Pure Land, Sukhavati)
The Pure Land of Amitabha Buddha. Many buddhists aspire to be reborn so they may cultivate diligently until reaching enlightenment, without fear of falling back into the six realms of reincarnation.

-X-

-Y-

Yaksa
A demon similar to a raksasa. Some are benevolent, like in the case of the twelve yaksas who serve and protect the Medicine Buddha. They aid and protect those who cultivate the Medicine Buddha Yoga. These twelve yaksas represent the twelve vows of the Medicine Bud-

dha.

Yamantaka (Sanskrit, literally "Conqueror of Death")
Commonly depicted with either a bull or buffalo head, he is the wrathful form of Manjushri Bodhisattva.

Yin and Yang
An ancient Chinese philosophy which explains how our universe is. It is the basis of Chinese medicine, martial arts, divination techniques, and Taoism. Yin refers feminine, cold, and dark while yang is masculine, hot, and light. They are polar opposites, neither good nor bad, which come together to create balance.

-Z-

Also From US Daden Culture

Sheng-yen Lu Book Collection 163:
Crossing the Ocean of Life and Death
Sale Price: US $12.00 dollars
ISBN:0-9841561-0-0

Sheng-yen Lu Book Collection 148:
The Power of Mantra
Sale Price: US $12.00 dollars
ISBN:0-9841561-1-9

Sheng-yen Lu Book Collection 154:
The Aura of Wisdom
Sale Price: US $12.00 dollars
Will publish in September 2010

3440 Foothill Blvd. • Oakland CA 94601 • U.S.A. • www.usdader